WINNING

VOLLEYBALL

DRILLS

Second Edition

Allen E. Scates

University of California, Los Angeles

wcb

Wm. C. Brown Publishers
2460 Kerper Blvd.
Dubuque, Iowa 52001

Photo credits

Chapter 1: Norm Schindler, ASUCLA
Chapter 2: Norm Schindler, ASUCLA
Chapter 3: Norm Schindler, ASUCLA
Chapter 4: Norm Schindler, ASUCLA
Chapter 5: Norm Schindler, ASUCLA
Chapter 6: Norm Schindler, ASUCLA
Chapter 7: George S. Yamashita
Chapter 8: Norm Schindler, ASUCLA
Chapter 9: Brian Kamper

Cover © David Madison 1988

Copyright © 1984, 1989 by Wm. C. Brown Publishers. All rights
reserved

Library of Congress Catalog Card Number: 88–71255

ISBN 0–697–08477–9

Printed in the United States of America by Wm. C. Brown Publishers
2460 Kerper Boulevard, Dubuque, IA 52001

10 9 8 7 6 5 4 3 2 1

ABOUT THE AUTHOR

UCLA HEAD VOLLEYBALL COACH
   NCAA CHAMPIONS 1970, '71, '72, '74, '75, '76, '79, '81, '82, '83, '84, '87
   Undefeated Seasons 1979 (31-0), 1982 (29-0), 1984 (38-0)
   1984 and 1987 NCAA Coach of the Year
   NCAA Runner Ups 1978, '80
   USVBA Collegiate Champions 1965, 1967
   USVBA Collegiate Runner Ups 1963, '64, '66, '69
   UCLA Coaching Record, 701 Wins, 101 Losses (.874)
   NCAA Tournament Record, 34 Wins, 3 Losses (.919)
HEAD COACH USVBA OPEN CHAMPIONS 1977, '78, '82
HEAD COACH 1971 U.S. PAN AMERICAN TEAM
HEAD COACH 1972 U.S. OLYMPIC TEAM
PLAYING RECORD
   USVBA Champions 1963, '64, '69, '78, '80, '86
   USVBA Runner Ups 1965, '67, '70, '77, '79
   USVBA First Team All American 1965, '77, '78, '79
   USVBA Second Team All American 1967, '80
   USVBA Honorable Mention 1966, '68
OWNER-DIRECTOR AL SCATES VOLLEYBALL CAMPS
CHAIRMAN MEN'S VOLLEYBALL COMMITTEE, AMERICAN VOLLEYBALL COACHES ASSOCIATION
MEMBER REEBOK SPORTS ADVISORY BOARD
MEMBER NATIONAL VOLLEYBALL TEAM REVIEW COMMITTEE

Contents

Preface

Over forty new drills that were originally tested by the 1987 UCLA, NCAA Champions have been included in this revision. The UCLA Team switched from a 6-2 to a 5-1 side out offense and most of the new drills reflect changes in passing, setting, and attack patterns that perfect our one setter offense. This revision also puts increased emphasis on correct movement patterns that enable the player to get to the ball efficiently. I want to thank Coaches Harlan Cohen, Wally Martin, and the UCLA players for the many hours they put in on the practice floor to perfect these drills.

A key to winning volleyball is conducting practice sessions using a wide variety of fundamental drills that change frequently enough to interest and motivate the athletes. Nothing is quite as boring to the athlete as using the same old drills over and over again. The drills that have been selected here allow the coach to teach the same techniques and tactics that the players will use in competition. The quality and quantity of drills in each chapter permit frequent change. It is most likely that every drill in this book will be used by the UCLA team at least once during any given season.

SYMBOLS

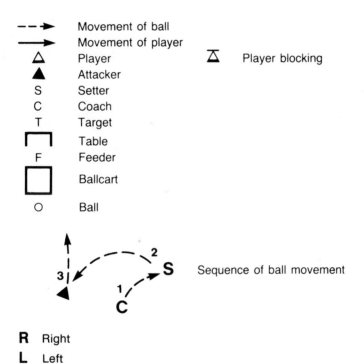

- – – ➤   Movement of ball
- ⟶   Movement of player
- △   Player   △̅   Player blocking
- ▲   Attacker
- S   Setter
- C   Coach
- T   Target
- ⊓   Table
- F   Feeder
- ☐   Ballcart
- O   Ball

Sequence of ball movement

R   Right

L   Left

1

Serve and Pass

DRILL 1-1 FOREARM PASS WITH SLIDE STEP

Purpose:
To teach the passer to move laterally using a "slide step" to position himself behind the ball.

Description:
Two tossers, each with a ball, stand with their back to the net and two-hand underhand toss the ball to the passer. The passer moves from side to side, stepping laterally, first with the outside foot and quickly sliding the trailing foot towards the lead foot. This action is repeated until the passer lines up with the oncoming ball whereupon the feet stop and the passer directs the ball back to the first tosser. The second tosser lets his ball go and the passer slides toward him. The action is repeated until the ball is contacted a specified number of times by the passer whereupon the passer becomes a tosser.

Coaching Tips:
The passer should be coached to stop the feet before the ball is contacted even if his body is not behind the ball. This will enable the passer to better control the forearm placement. This drill is for all levels from elementary school to college.

Equipment and Personnel:
Three players and two balls.

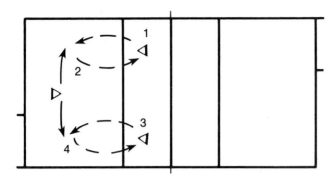

Figure 1-1   *Forearm Pass with Slide Step*

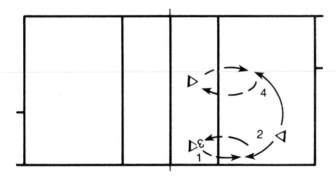

Figure 1-2   *Forearm Pass with Shuffle Step*

DRILL 1-2 FOREARM PASS WITH SHUFFLE STEP

Purpose:
To teach the passer to move laterally and forward without crossing the legs. This enables the passer better body control and should result in a better pass.

Description:
Two tossers stand with their backs to the net and alternately toss the ball to the passer. The passer is in a serve receiving position and quickly moves towards the tossed ball stepping with his outside foot first. The passer quickly returns to the starting position after the pass and then reacts to the next tossed ball. We time this drill and have each of the three players pass for four minutes.

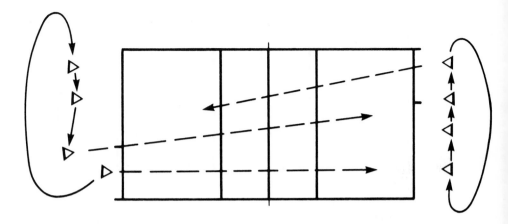

Figure 1-3 *Serving Drill*

Coaching Tips:
A wall and a line can be used to simulate a net and a sideline if there are not enough courts. Make sure that the passer moves quickly and stops with the feet further than shoulder width apart to provide a wide base of support for better balance. Use this drill at the beginning of every season; proper footwork is important.

Equipment And Personnel:
Three players and two balls.

DRILL 1-3 SERVING TECHNIQUE

Purpose:
To serve the ball in the opponent's court nine out of ten times while the coach corrects any errors in technique. At the beginning of the season every-one's serving technique must be checked by the coach to prevent the players from practicing mistakes.

Description:
Players serve and then move to the end of the serving line to retrieve balls coming from the other side of the net. Players do not serve until they rotate within the serving area located 9 feet 10 inches (3M) from the right sideline. The players should stand outside the court and signal to the server whether the ball is in or out on close plays.

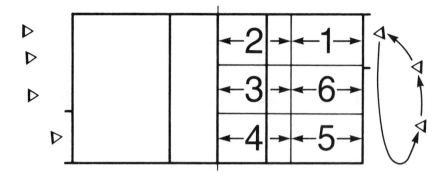

Figure 1-4   *Serving Specific Areas*

Coaching Tips:
Watch for the following in sequence: 1) toss in front of the striking shoulder; 2) elbow forward prior to contact; 3) a minimum of body rotation; 4) contact with the *heel* of the hand.

Equipment and Personnel:
Six to twelve players with one ball for every two people.

DRILL 1-4 SERVING SPECIFIC AREAS

Purpose:
To improve accuracy of the serve which will enable the server to use tactical placement in competition.

Description:
The court is divided into six equal areas according to the following numbers which are used internationally; area 1 = right back; area 2 = right forward; area 3 = center forward; area 4 = left forward; area 5 = left back; area 6 = center back. The coach assigns areas of the court for the servers to hit. Competition between courts will make the drill more interesting.

Coaching Tip:
Point the front foot in the direction of the intended target area.

Equipment and Personnel:
Six to twelve players with one ball for every two people. Towels, cones, ballcarts, tables, or chairs may be placed on the court for targets.

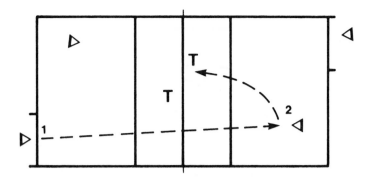

Figure 1-5   *Three Point Drill*

DRILL 1-5 THREE POINT DRILL

Purpose:
To serve and pass in a game situation.

Description:
The server and the passer play a game to three. The target (T) player is the referee. In order to win, the passer must deliver three good passes in a row to the target area. If the server serves out of the designated area or makes an error, it is a point for the passer. The server wins when the passer does not deliver the ball within the target area three times in a row. A 2-0 game for the server becomes 0-1 for the passer when a serve is passed into the specified target area. The target player takes the position of the winning player so that the losing player can continue to work on his technique.

Coaching Tip:
Designate a small target area if your team is using combination plays.

Equipment and Personnel:
Two balls and six players to a court.

DRILL 1-6 PARTNER PASSING

Purpose:
To practice receiving passes with the same player you will be next to in actual competition.

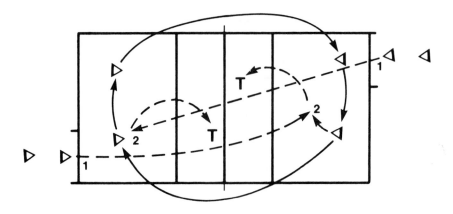

Figure 1-6   *Partner Passing*

Description:

The servers alternate and serve to areas 5, 6, or 1. The two passers must call for the serve and decide who will pass the ball that is between them. The ball is passed to the target player or coach who throws it back to the server on his side of the court. The four passers rotate one time in a clockwise manner so that the area 5 passer rotates to area 1 and the area 1 passer rotates to area 5. In a two-setter system all possible backcourt passing combinations will be covered in two rotations.

Coaching Tips:

The coach should designate which player takes the "seam" or area midway between the two passers in all receiving combinations. Players should be instructed to call "Mine!" for every ball they wish to receive.

Photo 1-1   *Partner Passing. When one player is a better passer than his backcourt teammate, he should be aggressive and receive most of the serves when that combination is together.* (Credit: Norm Schindler, ASUCLA)

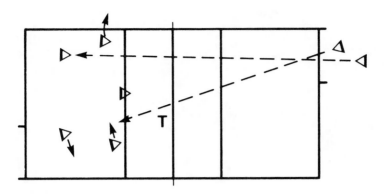

Figure 1-7   *Seam Serving and Pass*

Equipment and Personnel:

Eight to ten active players, two target players or coaches, and a ball for each server and target.

DRILL 1-7 SEAM SERVING AND PASS

Purpose:

To drill servers to make passers move for the ball and to condition passers to "call" for the serve reception.

Description:

Passers line up in their team serve receiving formation and practice calling for the ball on every serve. The servers' goal is to make the players move to reach the ball and force a bad pass. Players who are next to the passer should move away from the flight of the ball while watching for an errant pass as shown in Photo 1-2.

Coaching Tip:

Move away from the passer or "open the door" so that the player knows the serve is his responsibility.

Equipment and Personnel:

Four or five receivers, a target player, two or more servers, and four balls. This drill can be run on both sides of the net.

Photo 1-2   *Opening the Door. Karch pivots on his left foot to let the area 2 passer know he has the sole responsibility to receive the serve.* (Credit: Norm Schindler, ASUCLA)

DRILL 1-8 FRONTCOURT PASS AND SPIKE

Purpose:
To practice a side-out attack off of a short serve (See Photo 1-3).

Description:
The servers deliver the ball to area 2, 3, or 4 and the offense runs a side-out play or combination.

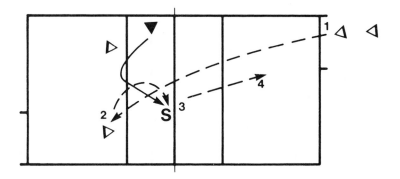

Figure 1-8   *Frontcourt Pass and Spike*

Photo 1-3   *The Table. Frontcourt passers should squat until their arms can be extended like a tabletop. This will send the ball high enough in the air to enable the passer/spiker to complete his approach and spike the ball. (Credit: Norm Schindler, ASUCLA)*

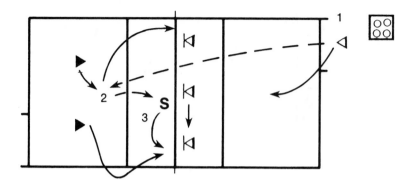

Figure 1-9   *Pass and Spike*

Coaching Tip:
Passers concentrate entirely on their pass and do not start their approach until the ball leaves their forearms.

Equipment and Personnel:
Two to six players can drill on siding out while the scoring team can be comprised of one server or a full defense.

DRILL 1-9 BACKCOURT PASS AND SPIKE

Purpose:
To train advanced players in the frontcourt rotations to back up and pass balls in the backcourt and approach and spike the set.

Description:
Two players pass the entire court and call for the type of set they want after determining the accuracy of the pass and their position after they pass. Blockers are optional in the beginning but should be added once the players begin passing accurately.

Coaching Tips:
The passer must call for *every* serve by yelling, ``Mine!''. The other player calls in or out.

Equipment and Personnel:
A ballcart with ten or more balls, two passers, a setter, and a server. Blockers and backcourt players are optional.

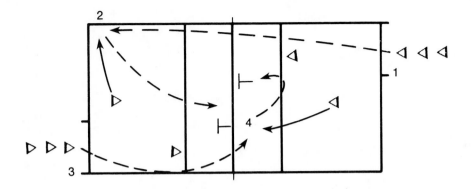

Figure 1-10 *Ace the Passer*

DRILL 1-10 ACE THE PASSER

Purpose:
To train an advanced passer to cover more territory when serve receiving and to teach the servers to keep the ball away from the passer.

Description:
One primary passer and one frontcourt passer cover the entire court. The frontcourt passer is only allowed to cover serves falling in area 2 and the other passer covers the remainder of the court. The servers attempt to ace the passer by hitting the deep corners or short frontcourt areas.

Coaching Tips:
Use this drill before playing an opponent with one primary passer who takes most of the serves. Have the first team serve against the quickest reserve passer.

Equipment and Personnel:
One ball for each server and four to twelve players.

2

Setting

DRILL 2-1 COACH CALLS THE SET

Purpose:
To make sure the setter and hitter know the names and routes of all the
sets in your offense.

Description:
The coach tosses the ball over the net to either of two passers who direct
the ball to the setter. As the ball is being passed, the coach yells the name of the
set and the spiker takes the appropriate route. The action is repeated until the
coach checks out the height and speed of all the sets in the offense.

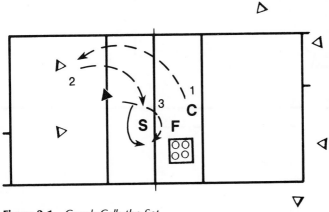

Figure 2-1 *Coach Calls the Set*

Coaching Tip:

The coach tosses balls that can be passed accurately and then focuses on the setter's feet to make sure that the right foot is slightly forward and pointed toward the antenna in area 4 when the ball is released.

Equipment and Personnel:

Four shaggers, a feeder, a coach, one hitter, one setter, and at least ten balls.

DRILL 2-2 FOUR-CORNER DRILL

Purpose:

To practice setting high balls to outside hitting positions.

Description:

The players in the backcourt deliver a high set to area 2 or 4; then the frontcourt player delivers a high set along the net before the ball is sent to the backcourt again. The difficulty can be increased when the pass to the backcourt causes the player in area 1 or 5 to dive, roll, or sprawl before bump setting to the frontcourt.

Coaching Tips:

Shape the hands to conform to the surface of the ball or, put more simply, SHAPE! Bend the legs and extend as the ball is released to set long distances.

Equipment and Personnel:

One ball and four players on each side of the net.

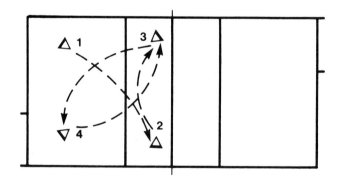

Figure 2-2   *Four-Corner Setting Drill (one ball)*

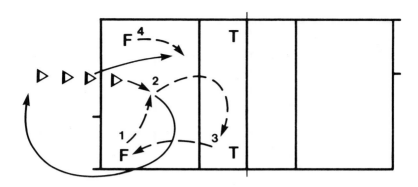

Figure 2-3   *Setting from Area 6 (two balls)*

DRILL 2-3 SETTING FROM AREA 6 (TWO BALLS)

Purpose:
To train the middle back player to set high to the corners of the net.

Description:
Two target/players (T) are placed in the front corners of the court by the net and two feeder/players (F) are placed near the endline and sideline. Four players form a line in area 6 by the endline and react to the balls the feeders deliver to them. The players call "Mine!" and deliver a high set to one of the target players and return to the end of the line as the target player quickly sets a low ball back to the feeder for continuous action. The feeders control the intensity of the drill by first giving the players balls they can set overhand and then increasing the players' range — causing them to bump set and finally dive and role to bump set the ball.

Coaching Tips:
Get to the ball as quickly as possible and set from a stationary position whenever you can.

Equipment and Personnel:
Two balls and eight players.

DRILL 2-4 THREE-PERSON BACKSET

Purpose:
To train players to set backsets and 30-foot sets.

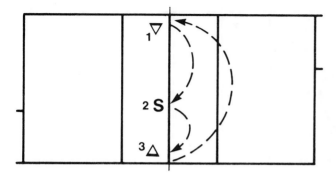

Figure 2-4 *Elementary Backset Drill*

Description:

The setter stands close to the net between two players standing on the sidelines and backsets the ball whenever it is passed to him; the player receiving the backset sets to the opposite sideline and that player passes the ball to the setter and the drill is repeated. Change the sequence halfway through the drill when middle blockers are in the setting (S) position so they will practice setting in both directions.

Coaching Tips:

Arch the back and extend the hands behind the head toward the target. The player receiving the backset comments on the placement to the setter who will continue to strive for improvement.

Equipment and Personnel:

Three players and one ball.

DRILL 2-5 MOCK BLOCK AND SET

Purpose:

To practice a quick recovery from blocking to setting.

Description:

The coach yells ''Block!'' and the area 2 player jumps and then lands on the outside foot and pivots toward the coach to see where he will pass the ball. The player moves to the ball, sets to area 4, and then follows his set to become the target player (T).

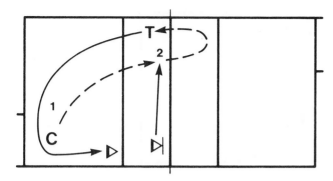

Figure 2-5 *Mock Block and Set*

Coaching Tips:
The coach should move all over the court and toss the ball so that the setter has to run, dive, roll, or sprawl to deliver the set. Occasionally the coach should be on the sideline in area 1 so that the setter can practice pivoting on the inside foot to look for the ball.

Equipment and Personnel:
Three to six players and one ball.

DRILL 2-6 BLOCK AND SET

Purpose:
To keep the eyes open while blocking to determine which way to pivot to go to the ball and set.

Description:
The coach (C) yells "Block!" and the area 2 player attempts to block as the coach spikes the ball over him at the area 1 digger. The blocker returns to the floor and sets the dug ball to the target player (T) in area 4.

Coaching Tips:
If your starting setter is blocking, instruct him to tilt the wrists and fingers back to "soft block" to prevent sprained or broken fingers. The soft block also speeds up the drill as most spikes are deflected to the area 1 digger.

Equipment and Personnel:
A table, coach, feeder, digger, blocker/setter, and target player.

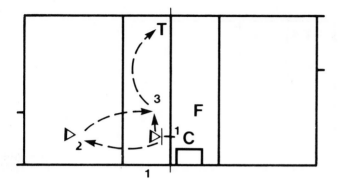

Figure 2-6 *Block and Set*

Variation:
A spiker can be substituted for the target player and up to six defensive players can be added.

DRILL 2-7 SPIKE OR JUMPSET

Purpose:
To add diversity to the offense.

Description:
The coach (C) yells ''Block!'' and the two players in area 2 mock block, then back off the net for an approach as the coach throws the ball to the area 2 hitter. The hitter has the option of spiking or setting to either of his frontcourt teammates depending on the reaction of the opponent middle blocker.

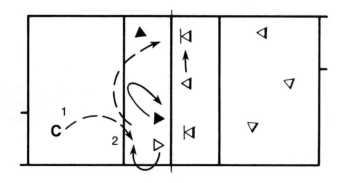

Figure 2-7 *Spike or Jump Set*

a

b

c

d

Photo 2-1 *The Jump Set. The setter uses a spike approach and after takeoff turns his shoulders at a 90-degree angle to the net (see Photo 2-1a) as the ball descends into his hands. Because the feet are off the floor, the power has to be generated solely by the arms and for that reason the ball should drop lower than the head (see Photo 2-1b) to give the elbows greater flexion for increased power, particularly on long sets. As the ball is released, the arms follow through toward the target.* (Credit: The Ealing Corporation)

Coaching Tip:
The area 2 spiker should hit the ball when only one blocker opposes him.

Equipment and Personnel:
This drill can be run with as few as seven players or as many as twelve if a full defense is used.

DRILL 2-8 RUN FORWARD, SET BACK

Purpose:
To train the setter to confuse the middle blocker by delivering a difficult set.

Description:
The setter starts in area 2 at the net and reacts to the pass by the coach. The pass is thrown into area 4 so the setter contacts the ball on the run and sets over his head to area 2. When the setter blocks in area 4, the drill can be run in the other direction; that is, the setter starts in area 4 and the coach tosses the ball in area 2. The setter turns and follows the set and becomes the target player who passes the set to the coach.

Coaching Tips:
Setters arch the back and neck while the hands follow through over the head.

Equipment and Personnel:
Two to six setters and one ball.

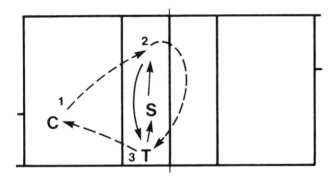

Figure 2-8   *Run Forward, Set Back (Setters)*

Photo 2-2 *The Jump Backset. One of the more difficult sets is a jump backset. The frontcourt setter above has taken the middle blocker out of the play with the threat of an attack and has set the ball to an outside hitter.* (Credit: Norm Schindler, ASUCLA)

DRILL 2-9 RUN BACKWARD, SET FORWARD

Purpose:
To train the setter to confuse the middle blocker by delivering a difficult set.

Description:
The setter starts in the seam of area 2/3 next to the net. The coach tosses the ball close to the right sideline, and the setter runs backward and sets the ball to area 4. The setter follows the set and becomes the target for the next player and then returns to the setting line.

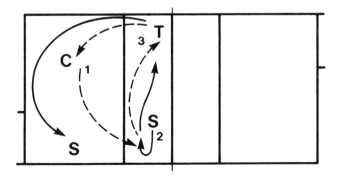

Figure 2-9 *Run Backward, Set Front (Setters)*

Coaching Tips:

The setter should run to the ball as quickly as possible and try to stop the feet and bend and extend the legs during the set. The setter's body should be moving toward the target as the ball is released.

Equipment and Personnel:

Three to six setters and one ball.

DRILL 2-10 SET A LOW PASS

Purpose:

To increase the setter's ability to set low passes.

Description:

The coach tosses low passes to try to define the limit of the setter's ability to set overhand legally and effectively. The setter must quickly judge whether to use the bump or overhand setting technique. The drill can emphasize front or back sets or combinations.

Coaching Tips:

The coach should extend the ability of the setter to take low balls overhand during the pre-season through use of this drill. As the season starts, the setter should know when to use the overhand or bump set in game situations. Each setter will have a different overhand range, and the coach should help the setter acknowledge this realistically.

Equipment and Personnel:

One ball and two to six setters.

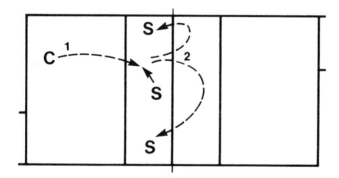

Figure 2-10   *Set a Low Pass*

Photo 2-3 *Setting from the knees. It is often desirable for the setter to drop to a low position to give the quick hitter time to jump for the set.* (Credit: Norm Schindler, ASUCLA)

DRILL 2-11 SET AND DIVE, ROLL OR SPRAWL

Purpose:
To practice setting erratic passes.

Description:
The coach tosses balls outside the setter's standing range to cause him to deliver the set from a variety of off-balance positions which cause him to go to the floor during or after the set.

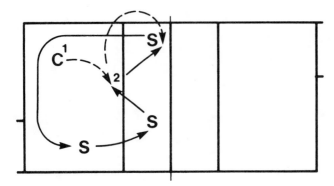

Figure 2-11 *Set and Dive, Roll or Sprawl*

Coaching Tips:
As the pass drops further away from the net, the height of outside sets should be increased to build a "margin of error" in the offense.

Equipment and Personnel:
One ball and three to six setters.

Photo 2-4 *Getting Low. It is possible for outstanding setters to deliver the ball accurately from a variety of positions.* (Credit: Richard Mackson)

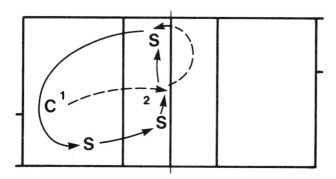

Figure 2-12 *Set Balls Passed over the Net*

DRILL 2-12 SET BALLS PASSED OVER THE NET

Purpose:
To become proficient at setting all combinations with passes that are flying over the net.

Description:
The coach throws balls over the net and the setter jump sets to various locations designated by the coach. Spikers and blockers may be added to the drill and plays and combinations practiced with passes that are flying over the net.

Coaching Tips:
The quick hitter should be up fast on a high close pass because the setter can easily give him a one-hand set as shown in Photo 2-5.

Equipment and Personnel:
One to six setters and one ball. The drill may also be run with two full teams and several balls.

Photo 2-5 *One-Hand Set. No. 1 is preparing to take off to hit a quick set as Karch Kiraly (No. 31) is about to "tee up" the ball for him.* (Credit: Norm Schindler, ASUCLA)

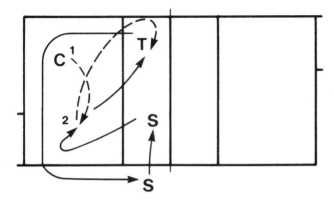

Figure 2-13   *Set Deep Passes (Setters)*

DRILL 2-13 SET DEEP PASSES

Purpose:
To accurately set the offense when the ball is passed ten feet and more from the net.

Description:
The setter starts at the net and the coach passes balls deep into his court. The setter runs the ball down, passes to the target player, then acts as the target for the next setter before returning the ball to the coach and setting again.

Coaching Tips:
When the setters become proficient at setting deep passes to the outside, start running combination plays as shown in Photo 2-6. If the setter can connect with the quick hitter on a bad pass, then one-on-one situations are still possible.

Equipment and Personnel:
One to six setters and one ball. Add spikers and blockers later.

Photo 2-6   *The Deep Right Cross. No. 1 prepares to take off for the quick set as the setter contacts the ball above the attack line. No. 23 circles behind the setter in a deep crossing pattern to take off behind No. 1.* (Credit: Norm Schindler, ASUCLA)

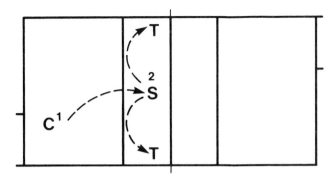

Figure 2-14   *Command Set (Setters)*

DRILL 2-14 COMMAND SET

Purpose:
To release every set above the head so that the opposing blockers cannot "read" the set and get a jump on the attackers.

Description:
The coach tosses the ball to the setter and shouts "Front" or "Back" just as the setter contacts the ball.

Photo 2-7   *Release Point. An accomplished setter can release sets in any direction from the same position and thus will prevent two blockers from being at the point of attack.* (Credit: Norm Schindler, ASUCLA)

Coaching Tips:

Release the ball above the head on front, back, and quick sets. Most setters let the ball drop in front of them for a forward set and only contact the ball above their head when setting back.

Equipment and Personnel:

One to six setters and one to two balls.

DRILL 2-15 ATTACK THE PASS

Purpose:

To make the setter an offensive threat by hitting, dumping, or jamming the pass into or over the block.

Description:

The coach passes balls above the net until the setters can use their left and right hand effectively to spike and dump the pass into the opponents' court. Next, blockers and attackers are added to the drill, and the setter has the option of attacking or setting depending on the reaction of the blocker opposite him.

Coaching Tips:

Spend a lot of time teaching the setter to use the left hand (see Photo 2-8) because the athlete does not have to change body position for a left-handed jam when facing area 4. It is quicker and more deceptive than a right-handed spike.

Equipment and Personnel:

One to six setters and several balls.

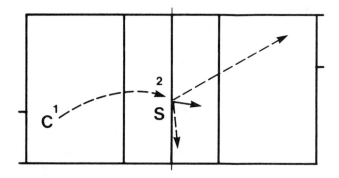

Figure 2-15 *Attack the Pass*

Photo 2-8 *Left-hand Jam. The setter (No. 11) elects to dump the ball with his left hand as the quick hitter is taking off.* (Credit: Norm Schindler, ASUCLA)

DRILL 2-16 SET AND BLOCK

Purpose:
To develop a quick transition from offense to defense.

Description:
A coach stands on each side of the net in area 1 and tosses a ball to the setter after he blocks. The setter delivers the ball to the hitter in area 4 and follows the set, then returns to area 2 to block the opponent's spike. These two actions by the setter are quickly repeated over and over until the coach substitutes new setters into the drill.

Coaching Tip:
The setter should pivot on one foot as he lands from blocking and face the backcourt as No. 11 in Photo 2-9 demonstrates.

Equipment and Personnel:
Eight balls and two setters; two to six spikers.

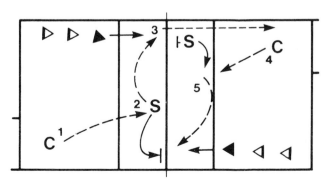

Figure 2-16 *Set and Block*

Photo 2-9   *Setter in Transition. No. 11 is coming off the block to receive the dig and run the offense.* (Credit: Norm Schindler, ASUCLA)

DRILL 2-17 DIG AND SET

Purpose:
To dig a spike and set to area 4.

Description:
The coach stands in area 4 and spikes to the setter in area 1 or 2. The nondigging player sets the ball back to the coach and the action is repeated.

Coaching Tip:
The setter in area 2 digs the ball high to give the backcourt setter time to penetrate toward the net.

Equipment and Personnel:
One coach, two setters, and an optional feeder if the diggers have poor control. If they have good control, use one ball and delete the feeder.

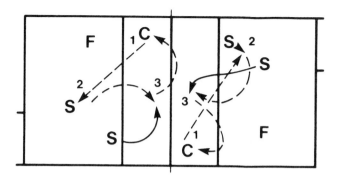

Figure 2-17   *Dig and Set*

DRILL 2-18 SETTING THE A—CLOSE PASS

Purpose:
To introduce the A set under perfect conditions.

Description:
The coach passes the ball right to the setter who stands close to the net. The spiker runs to the setter and takes off as the setter prepares to release the ball. There is very little broadjumping after the takeoff.

Photo 2-10 *Setting the A — Close Pass. The spiker should always expect a jump set on a close pass and be prepared to spike the ball inches from the setter's fingertips.* (Credit: Norm Schindler, ASUCLA)

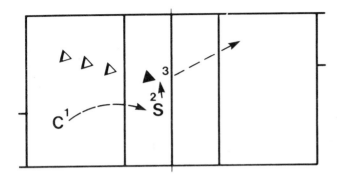

Figure 2-18   *Setting the A — Close Pass*

Coaching Tips:
The setter should jump set all close high passes to cut down the time between her release and the spiker contacting the ball. The ball should be set vertically, slightly backward from the net at a height to give the spiker a chance to use a fully extended armswing.

Equipment and Personnel:
Four balls and five to twelve players.

DRILL 2-19 SETTING THE A—MEDIUM PASS

Purpose:
To work on the timing between setter and hitter using the type of passes that are likely to occur in game conditions.

Description:
The coach lobs passes to the setter from four to eight feet from the net anywhere on the court. The spiker runs to the setter and takes off alongside her and broadjumps toward the net. The setter delivers a high fast set to make the hitter fully extend her arm. If they miss connections the ball should fly over the net and be kept in play.

Coaching Tip:
The spiker should "open up" to the setter by placing her shoulders at a 90 degree angle to the net as shown in Photo 2-11. This increases the spiker's range and allows her to hit poor sets.

Equipment and Personnel:
Four balls and five to twelve players.

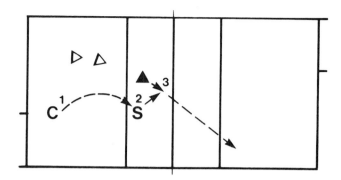

Figure 2-19   *Setting the A — Medium Pass*

Photo 2-11   *Setting the A — Medium Pass. Since the setter is not close to the net and cannot fool the blockers with a jump set, she keeps both feet on the floor. No. 2 is broad-jumping toward the net and No. 10 must set laterally toward the net and keep the set in front of the moving attacker. (Credit: Norm Schindler, ASUCLA)*

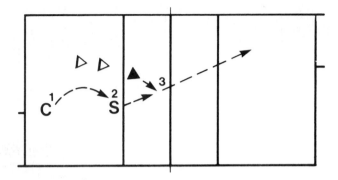

Figure 2-20   *Setting the A — Deep Pass*

DRILL 2-20 SETTING THE A—DEEP PASSES

Purpose:
To surprise the opponents' block with a quick set to the middle attacker on a bad pass. When the offense can connect on a few of these plays, it will hold the middle blocker and it may still be possible to get a one-on-one situation using the outside attackers. The deep A set is a difficult play and should only be used in competition after successful training.

Description:
The coach passes balls from sideline to sideline around the attack line. The spiker runs by the setter and takes off well in front of him (see Photo 2-12) and broadjumps toward the net.

Coaching Tip:
The setter must set the ball with as much velocity as he can on a deep A set or the timing with the spiker will be poor. Most setters slow the set down when the pass is bad and do not connect with the spiker who is used to taking off as the setter touches the ball.

Equipment and Personnel:
Four balls and five to twelve players.

Photo 2-12   *Setting the A – Deep Pass. Karch Kiraly (No. 31) has dropped to a full squat to set a low, deep pass to Steve Salmons. The set is going to be fast to give Steve a chance to go one-on-one with the middle blocker and high so that it will cross into the opponents' court even if they miss connections.* (Credit: Norm Schindler, ASUCLA)

DRILL 2-21 SETTING THE C

Purpose:
To split the area 2 and 3 blocker with a quick set to the middle attacker that is hit six to eight feet from the setter.

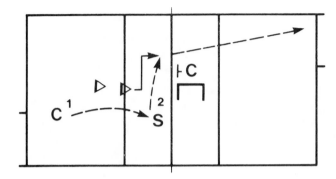

Figure 2-21   *Setting the C*

Description:

The coach passes to the setter who sets a quick flat set to the middle attacker. The height of the set depends on the reach and jumping ability of the attacker. The attacker hits away from the middle blocker into area 1. A blocker or assistant coach can stand on a table about eleven feet from the sideline to force the spiker to cut back to area 1.

Coaching Tip:

In competition the area 4 spiker must be alert in case the set is missed by the quick hitter so he can hit the ball over the net.

Equipment and Personnel:

Four balls, a table, and six to nine players.

Photo 2-13   *The C Set. Steve Salmons jumps ten feet from the sideline to hit a high fast three set which has left the opposition on the floor. (Credit: Norm Schindler, ASUCLA)*

3

Spiking Drills

DRILL 3-1 FOUR STEP APPROACH

Purpose:
To teach the players the best footwork to use when there is time for a long approach.

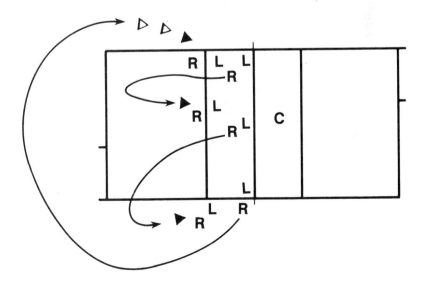

Figure 3-1 *Four-Step Approach*

Description:

The spiker lines up behind the three meter line and steps on the tape the coach has placed on the court. The letter R for right foot is taped for the first step; L for the second, R for the third and L for the final step. The steps increase in length from the first to the last step. The lengths of the steps depend on the age and size of the team. Stronger and bigger players take larger steps. Use three lines on each court.

Coaching Tip:

Tell the players to increase their speed and use a two foot take off with proper arm action and simulate the spike.

Equipment and Personnel:

Tape that does not remove varnish or paint. Use one coach for every court.

DRILL 3-2 THREE STEP APPROACH

Purpose:

To teach the players the best footwork to use when spiking a low outside set or when making quick transitions from defense to offense.

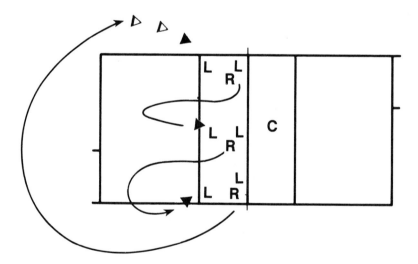

Figure 3-2   *Three-Step Approach*

Description:

The spiker lines up even with the three meter line and uses a left foot, right foot, left foot approach. The coach puts tape on the floor and the spiker follows the diagram and simulates a spike without the ball.

Coaching Tips:

The three step approach should be used when receiving a low fast set. When the outside hitter sees the setter receive a good pass he should yell, "Quick," "Shoot," or some other verbal signal to insure a low fast set to beat the middle blocker. Tape and one coach per court.

DRILL 3-3 APPROACH FOR THE A SET

Purpose:

To learn deceptive footwork to quickly position a middle spiker in front of the setter.

Description:

The quick hitter moves in line with the setter as the setter receives the pass. The hitter then takes the first step at the setter with the right foot and pushes off the left foot on the second step to veer in front of the setter as the right foot hits the floor on the third step. The fourth and final step with the left foot is used to brake the forward momentum and to help turn the body towards the setter to put the striking arm in position to hit the one or A set.

Coaching Tips:

Make sure the spikers jump several feet from the center line so they can broad jump toward the net before contacting the set. After the spikers can step on the tape on the floor, introduce the ball and have the spikers hit an A set.

Equipment and Personnel:

Tape, a setter, and one ball for every spiker.

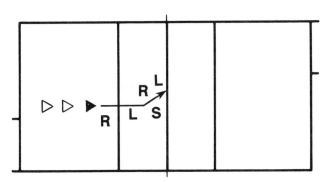

Figure 3-3 *Approach for the A Set*

Photo 3-1 *Hitting the A Set. Once the spiker uses the proper footwork and takeoff to get to the point of attack, she must raise her striking arm with her elbow about shoulder height as the setter releases the ball. She then swings quickly (using a minimum of body torque) to beat the blocker.* Credit Line: Norm Schindler.

DRILL 3-4 APPROACH FOR THE SLIDE SET

Purpose:

To learn to quickly position the right side attacker about three feet in front of the setter for a lob set.

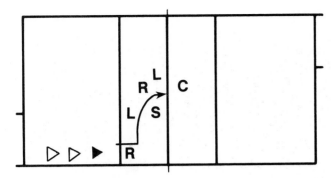

Figure 3-4 *Approach for the Slide Set*

Description:
The right side attacker stays on the right sideline to hold the end blocker in place and then with a burst of speed uses a four step approach to broadjump by the setter to hit a short lob set that is slower than an A set and faster than an X set.

Coaching Tip:
The longer the attacker waits before starting the approach the better the chance of beating the block.

Equipment and Personnel:
Tape, a setter and one ball for every spiker.

DRILL 3-5 APPROACH FOR THE B SET

Purpose:
To learn footwork to quickly position the spiker directly behind the setter.

Description:
The quick hitter moves in line with the setter as the setter receives the pass. The hitter then takes the first two steps of the four step approach directly at the setter before veering off to the right to hit a back one or B set.

Photo 3-2   *Hitting the Slide Set. It is very important that the spiker take her last step with the left foot so she can turn and face the setter to increase her range of effectiveness. Spikers who take the last step with the right foot will miss many sets because they cannot "open up" to the setter and block the set with the right shoulder.* Credit Line: Norm Schindler.

Coaching Tip:

The coach should pass the ball accurately to the setter to enable the spiker to concentrate on proper footwork during a controlled situation. When the spiker can change direction with the left foot on the second step and make good contact with the set the passer should be moved around the net.

Equipment and Personnel:

One setter and ball for each spiker.

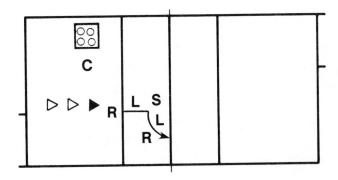

Figure 3-5 *Approach for the B Set*

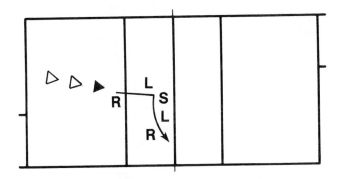

Figure 3-6 *Approach for the Flair Set*

DRILL 3-6 APPROACH FOR THE FLAIR SET

Purpose:
To learn footwork to enable the spiker to broad jump away from the setter for a set that is slower and a little wider than a B set.

Description:
The quick attacker uses a four step approach and takes the first two steps at the setter. The spiker then pushes off to the right on the second step and veers by the setter at a 45 degree angle to spike the flair set.

Coaching Tip:
The flair is a good set that the quick attacker can call for when he sees that a blocker is standing in front of the setter.

Equipment and Personnel:
One setter and ball for each spiker.

Photo 3-3   *Hitting the B Set. Since the setter cannot see the attacker when releasing the ball, the player must be sure to broad jump towards the net to increase the probability of the set being delivered between the spiker and the net. Most errors on this play occur because the spiker takes off too close to the net. Credit Line: George S. Yamashita.*

DRILL 3-7 MIDDLE APPROACH FOR THE C SET

Purpose:
To use footwork that quickly distances the middle attacker from the setter.

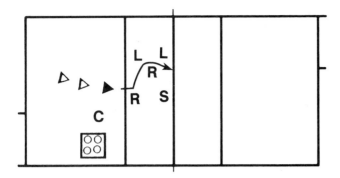

Figure 3-7 *Middle Approach for the C Set*

Description:
The quick hitter moves in line with the setter and then pivots on his right foot during the first step and jumps to the left before taking the third and fourth step towards the net. This will put the spiker in position to hit a quick set that travels five to seven feet from the setter to the attacker.

Coaching Tips:
The right-handed spiker must take the last step with the left foot so he can ''open'' his body towards the setter to give him an increased range of contact with the set. The spiker should hit the ball away from the middle blocker into area 1.

Equipment and Personnel:
One setter and a ball for each quick hitter.

DRILL 3-8 OUTSIDE APPROACH FOR THE C SET

Purpose:
To use footwork that quickly puts an outside hitter in position for a C set contacted five to eight feet from the setter.

Description:
The outside hitter starts near the left sideline behind the three meter line and takes the first step toward the setter with the right foot. The second step with the left foot is longer and faster and puts the spiker in front of the three meter line. The last two steps place the spiker five to eight feet from the setter at the net.

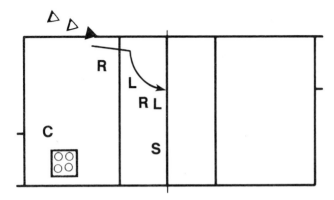

Figure 3-8   *Outside Approach for the C Set*

Coaching Tip:
Remind the outside hitter to start late and travel fast to give the blocker less time to react.

Equipment and Personnel:
One setter and a ball for each quick hitter.

DRILL 3-9 RAPID-FIRE SPIKING

Purpose:
To warm the players up and allow them to work on whatever spiking position they desire against one blocker.

Description:
There are three spiking lines, one setter, and one blocker. First the area 2, then 3 and 4 spikers pass the ball and spike in rapid order. The blocker blocks nine times (three trips across the net) and then a new blocker takes his place. The spikers shag their own spike and return to a spiking line.

Coaching Tip:
The coach can concentrate on watching the spiker's approach to make sure he waits long enough after the pass to approach fast for a maximum jump. If he leaves too soon, he will have to slow down for the set, which will decrease the jump.

Equipment and Personnel:
One ball for every spiker. Nine to twelve players to a court.

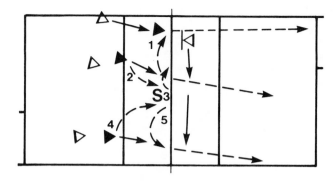

Figure 3-9 *Rapid-fire Spiking*

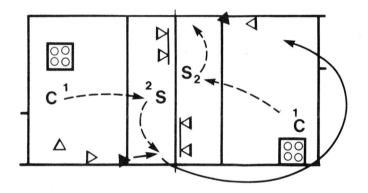

Figure 3-10 *Fives versus Two Blockers*

DRILL 3-10 FIVES VERSUS TWO BLOCKERS

Purpose:
To practice defeating a two-person block from area 2.

Description:
The coach passes to the setter who backsets to the area 2 spiker who is opposed by two blockers. After the spike the hitter shags the ball and puts it in the ballcart on the other side of the net.

Photo 3-4   *Eye on the Ball. Many players close their eyes and drop their heads just prior to contact. If the set is watched until contact is made, as demonstrated by Karch Kiraly above, the control will be greater.* (Credit: Norm Schindler, ASUCLA)

Coaching Tips:
Make sure the setter follows his set and backs up the hitter. In the event the ball is blocked, continue playing. *Never* let the blocked spike hit the floor; always attempt to play the ball.

Equipment and Personnel:
Two ballcarts, two coaches or feeders, and nine to twelve players.

DRILL 3-11 FOURS VERSUS TWO BLOCKERS

Purpose:
To train the ouside hitters with area 4 hitting assignments and to train the middle blockers and middle back defenders.

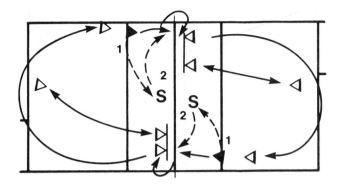

Figure 3-11 *Fours versus Two Blockers*

Description:

The outside hitters rotate clockwise, spiking, end blocking, shagging, and then passing and spiking again. The four middle blockers alternate playing middle back defense and blocking the middle every three minutes or so. Any player or the coach can set the low outside set called a four so that the setters can practice spiking.

Coaching Tip:

The spiker has to keep the set in front of her so that she can see the ball and the blockers. A common error is to run under the set and look up at the ball and lose sight of the blockers.

Equipment and Personnel:

Six balls, four middle blockers, two setters, and four to six outside hitters.

Photo 3-5 *Spiking a Four Set. The four set is designed to be low enough to reach the spiker before the middle blocker can reach the outside blocker. Both the middle and end blockers have unsuccessfully attempted to close the seam between them with lateral arm movements to prevent a hole in the block.* (Credit: George S. Yamashita)

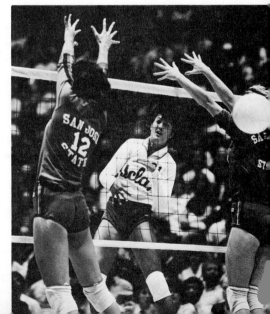

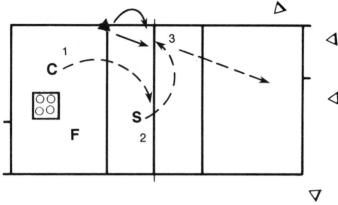

Figure 3-12   *Outside Hitter Audibilizing*

DRILL 3-12 OUTSIDE HITTER AUDIBILIZING

Purpose:
To teach the outside hitter to audibilize and change his spiking approach when anticipating a low, fast set.

Description:
The coach randomly alternates good tosses and bad tosses to the setter. When the attacker sees a good toss he calls, "Shoot" and the setter delivers a fast low set designed to beat the middle blocker. To hit a shoot set the spiker moves in front of the three meter line and moves outside the court using a three step approach. On a bad toss the setter delivers a four set and the spiker uses a four step approach.

Coaching Tips:
After the toss the coach watches the footwork of the attacker and makes sure he uses a wider route on the "shoot" set with a three step approach. This will enable the spiker to hit the ball sharply crosscourt since the middle blocker will probably be late on this set. The same drill should be run with the right side attacker.

Equipment and Personnel:
A ballcart with ten balls, four shaggers, a setter, a feeder, an attacker, and a coach.

Photo 3-6 *Spiking a Deep Set. Hitters cannot hit a deep set in a downward trajectory and must rely on top-spin to keep a hard spike inbounds.* (Credit: Norm Schindler, ASUCLA)

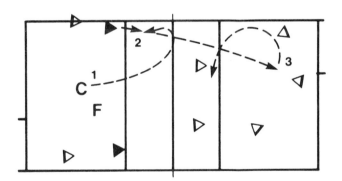

Figure 3-13 *Spike Deep Sets*

DRILL 3-13 SPIKE DEEP SETS

Purpose:

To drill spikers to swing hard at balls set off the net and keep the ball inbounds.

Description:

The spiker hits and then goes to the end of his spiking line. The coach alternates tossing deep sets from area 6 to the left and right spiking lines. Three diggers attempt to dig every spike and two shaggers retrieve the balls and return them to the feeder who stands next to the coach. The coach divides his group in half and rotates the two groups as a unit; that is, the diggers and shaggers become the spikers and feeder and vice versa.

Coaching Tips:
On a deep set the ball should be contacted above the spiking shoulder as demonstrated by Rick Amon in Photo 3-6; this contact position allows the spiker to first hit the ball below the midline and then quickly snap his wrist forward, imparting topspin to the ball. The topspin causes the ball to drop and increases the probability of a powerful spike staying inbounds.

Equipment and Personnel:
Six balls, ten to twelve players, and one coach.

DRILL 3-14 BACKCOURT SPIKING

Purpose:
To dig and spike balls that are set to backcourt attackers.

Description:
The coach initiates the drill by tossing the ball to the setter who delivers the set to either the right back or center back player. If the right back player wants the set he calls, "D"; if the center back player wants the set he calls "Pipe". The ball is set five to eight feet from the net and the attacker takes off behind the three meter line and tries to put the spike on the opponent's floor. The three diggers on the other side of the net dig the ball and call for the same sets. The diggers in area 1 do not call for the set unless the ball is dug to the player in area 4.

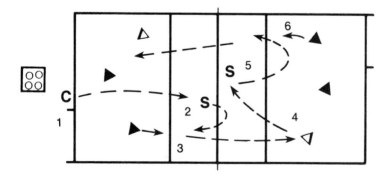

Figure 3-14 *Backcourt Spiking*

Coaching Tips:

Watch the spikers' take off and let them know when they step over the three meter line. They can still send the ball over the net but they cannot attack from above the net when they take off in front of the three meter line.

Equipment and Personnel:

Six digger-attackers, two setters, one coach, a ballcart, and ten balls.

DRILL 3-15 DINK TO THE TARGET

Purpose:

To place the dink shot to a specific point on the opponent's court.

Description:

The coach places a towel on the floor indicating where the spiker is to dink the ball. When drilling during the season, the towel is placed in the next opponent's vulnerable area. Generally the three areas in the diagram are enough to cover all defenses. Blockers are used so that the dink is not too low.

Coaching Tips:

The spiker is to approach late and fast and bend her arm in the usual spiking technique before slowing the arm down and looping the ball over the net with her fingertips.

Equipment and Personnel:

One towel, four balls, and six to nine players.

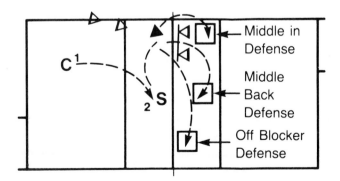

Figure 3-15   *Dink to the Target*

Photo 3-7   *The Dink Shot. The ball is contacted below the midline and lofted up and over blockers.* (Credit: Norm Schindler, ASUCLA)

DRILL 3-16 OFF-SPEED SHOTS

Purpose:
To loop a spike over the block to a vulnerable spot in the opponents' defense.

Description:
The off-speed spike is contacted with the palm of the hand and looped over the block. The target should be placed near the attack line in the center of the court to simulate the open area in the middle back defense. The spiker hits an off-speed shot, blocks twice, shags the ball, passes to the setter, and repeats.

Coaching Tip:
This shot is most effective when used by a hard spiker who uses the shot infrequently.

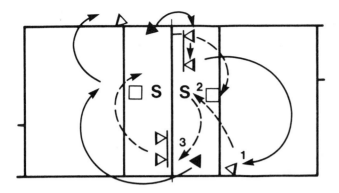

Figure 3-16 *Off-speed Shots*

Equipment and Personnel:
Two towels, six balls, and eight to twelve players.

DRILL 3-17 MOCK BLOCK AND SPIKE

Purpose:
To make the transition from blocking to spiking quickly and effectively.

Description:
1) The player jumps as if to block; 2) the coach throws the ball to the setter as the player reaches the apex of his block jump; 3) the player now quickly backs off the net to use an approach to spike; 4) the setter delivers a high outside set and the player tries to put the ball away against a two-person block and a middle back defender.

Coaching Tip:
Using a good middle back defender in spiking drills will let the attacker know he has to vary his shots rather than hitting off the middle blocker's hands.

Equipment and Personnel:
Five balls and six to ten players.

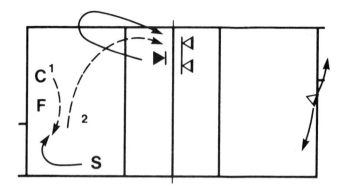

Figure 3-17   *Mock Block and Spike*

DRILL 3-18 SPIKE OVERSETS

Purpose:
To put away balls that are passed or set over the net.

Description:
Three blockers line up across the net from the coach who passes the ball over the net. The blockers then spike the ball to the floor. The coach varies his passes to simulate game conditions.

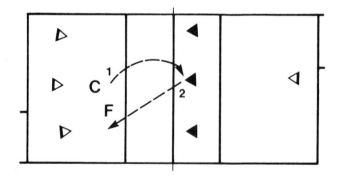

Figure 3-18   *Spike Oversets*

Photo 3-8 *Spiking Oversets. As unbe-lievable as it may seem, many fine players have difficulty in spiking a ball passed over the net and make errors even when un-opposed by a block. Rick Amon demon-strates the correct technique by jumping high and keeping his eyes on the ball.* (Credit: Norm Schindler, ASUCLA)

Coaching Tip:
Advanced players can work on jump setting to another spiker when the ball is passed too far from the net.

Equipment and Personnel:
Three balls, three blockers, at least four shaggers, and a passer or a coach.

DRILL 3-19 WIPE-OFF SHOT

Purpose:
To spike the ball off the end blocker's hand so that the defense cannot return it.

Description:
The feeder throws the ball on top of the net or one or two feet to either side. Two players on opposite sides of the net either block or spike wipe-off shots. The shagger returns the ball and the drill continues until one of the players gets three points. The feeder is also the referee and settles any disputes that may arise. The winner can stay in and play the feeder or two new players can start another game to three.

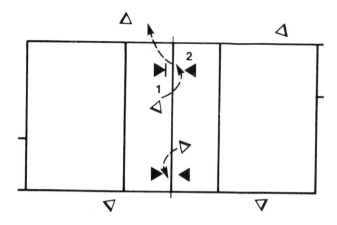

Figure 3-19   *Wipe-off Shot*

Coaching Tip:
Do not try a wipe-off shot against small blockers as they do not give the spiker enough area to hit.

Equipment and Personnel:
Two balls and six to twelve players.

Photo 3-9   *Wipe-off Shot. On a close set the spiker should swing laterally toward the closest sideline to hit the ball off the blocker's outside hand.* (Credit: Norm Schindler, ASUCLA)

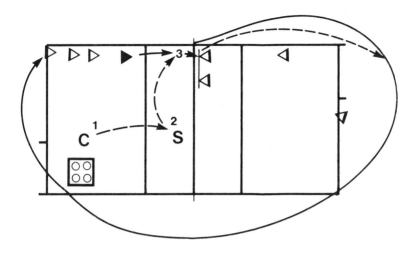

Figure 3-20 *The High Flat Shot*

DRILL 3-20 HIGH FLAT SHOT

Purpose:
To spike the ball off the top of the end blocker's fingers so that the ball sails over the area 1 digger and away from the area 6 digger.

Description:
The coach passes to the setter who sets to the area 4 attacker. The attacker hits straight ahead at the end blocker's hands, attempting to draw a touch on the blocker and make the ball land beyond the endline. The spiker then shags the ball, returns it to the cart, and spikes again. The coach switches the middle blocker and area 6 player as well as the area 2 blocker and area 1 defender. The defenders then switch places with the attackers.

Photo 3-10 *High Flat Shot. This spike rarely gets blocked for a point and will often score when hit down the line against a middle back defense.* (Credit: Norm Schindler, ASUCLA)

Coaching Tips:

A good blocker will occasionally drop his hands at the last instant, hoping the spiker will hit the high flat shot out of bounds. This move should be incorporated in the drill so that the spiker will recognize the ploy and spike downward into the court.

Equipment and Personnel:

Four balls and nine to twelve players.

DRILL 3-21 RIGHT CROSS—SPIKE TO AREA 5

Purpose:

To develop the offensive capability of cutting back to area 5 in the event an area 4 blocker is not up as shown in Photo 3-11.

Description:

The feeding line passes the ball to the setter. The area 2 spiker runs in for an X set and cuts back to area 5. The spiker then shags the ball and goes to the feeding line to pass for a teammate before spiking again.

Coaching Tip:

The setter should deliver an "up and down" or vertical set so the spiker can run by the ball to move the middle blocker toward area 2.

Equipment and Personnel:

Six balls and eight to twelve players.

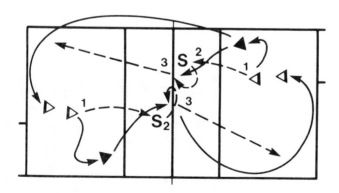

Figure 3-21 *Right Cross – Spike to Area 5*

Photo 3-11 *The X Spiker Hits to Area 5. The quick attacker is on the floor after jumping for a quick set which he did not receive. The area 4 blocker is also on the floor after jumping to block the quick hitter. The X spiker hits over the grounded blocker to area 5.* (Credit: Norm Schindler, ASUCLA)

DRILL 3-22 RIGHT CROSS—SPIKE TO AREA 1

Purpose:
To develop the offensive capability of spiking over the middle blocker when he has jumped with the quick hitter (see Photo 3-12 a,b,c,d).

Description:
The feeder passes to the setter who delivers an X set to the area 2 spiker who spikes into area 1. The spiker then shags the ball and goes into the feeding line.

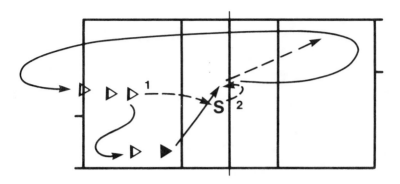

Figure 3-22   *Right Cross — Spike to Area 1*

a

b

c

d

Photo 3-12   *Right Cross — Spike to Area 1. The quick hitter in Photos 3-12 a,b,c has taken the middle blocker out of the play, allowing the setter to deliver an X set to the crossing area 2 spiker who hits into area 1 (Photo 3-12 d).* (Credit: Norm Schindler, ASUCLA, 3-12 a,b; Stan Troutman, ASUCLA, 3-12, c,d)

Coaching Tip:

During competition the spiker should watch the middle blocker, and if he jumps with the quick hitter, he should spike over him.

Equipment and Personnel:

Five balls and six to twelve players.

DRILL 3-23 FAKE CROSS

Purpose:

To take advantage of the area 4 blocker once the right cross has been established.

Description:

The feeder passes the ball to the setter. The area 2 spiker crosses behind the setter and then pushes off on his left foot to spike a backset in area 2. He then shags the ball and goes to the feeding line before spiking again.

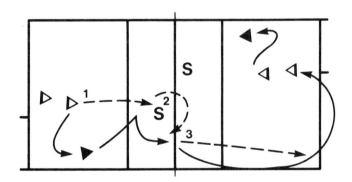

Figure 3-23   *Fake Cross*

Photo 3-13   *Fake Cross. The area 4 blocker has keyed on the quick hitter and is now riveted to the floor as the area 2 spiker is preparing to spike a backset over him.* (Credit: Norm Schindler, ASUCLA)

Coaching Tip:

Use a four-step approach: 1) step right; 2) left and then push off toward the sideline; 3) step right; and 4) close and take off when the left foot touches the floor.

Equipment and Personnel:

Six balls and eight to twelve spikers.

4

Blocking

There are normally only three times during team practice when spikers should be allowed to spike the ball without a block: 1) during the preseason when the spiker is working on approach and takeoff; 2) when new combination plays are being introduced; and 3) when players are warming up prior to a match. Even while warming up for a match we have used blockers to encourage thinking about game shots. In practice any time we are running a spiking drill, we are also running a blocking drill.

DRILL 4-1 PARTNER BLOCKING

Purpose:
To develop the blockers' movement technique and warm-up for blocking.

Description:
The blockers slide step across two nets and mock block three times along each net with their partner. This drill is done without a ball because the entire squad is involved. The drill simulates the action in Photo 4-1 except that the players push against each other's hands on top of the net rather than the ball. After each player has slide stepped two courts to her left and right, the drill can be repeated using the crossover step.

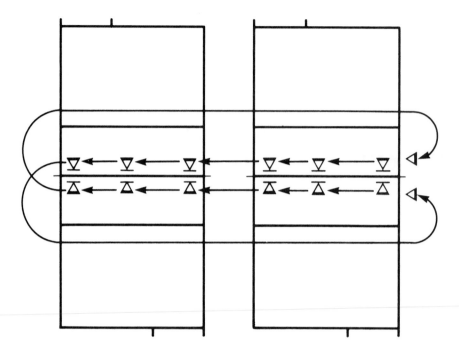

Figure 4-1   *Partner Blocking*

Coaching Tip:
Match the players up according to height and jumping ability so that everyone can use maximum block jumps to help increase power.

Equipment and Personnel:
Two courts and the entire squad.

DRILL 4-2 RAPID-FIRE BLOCKING

Purpose:
To warm up the players for spiking and blocking and to improve these two techniques.

Description:
One blocker faces three hitting lines and attempts to block the area 4, 3, and 2 hitters in rapid succession. The spikers pass their own balls as soon as the setter delivers the previous set to keep the blocker moving; each blocker makes

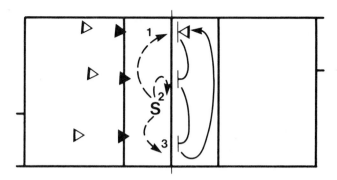

Figure 4-2 *Rapid-fire Blocking*

three trips across the front row until everyone blocks. The drill is usually repeated. The spikers shag their own balls and return to the hitting line of their choice.

Coaching Tip:

Watch the blocker's footwork and help him with any technical corrections immediately after his three trips across the net.

Equipment and Personnel:

Use all available courts and have one ball for each spiker.

DRILL 4-3 ONE-ON-ONE REPETITIVE BLOCKS

Purpose:

To learn to watch the spiker's body and arm to "read" the direction of the spike.

Description:

The coach stands on a table and repetitively spikes balls down the line or crosscourt. The coach turns his body in the direction of the intended spike so that the blocker learns to position himself according to the spiker's actions. The blocker rotates to feeder and then to shagger when the coach deems the player has had enough. Two drills can take place on the same court.

Coaching Tip:

Watch the blocker's eyes to make sure they are open when the spiker contacts the ball.

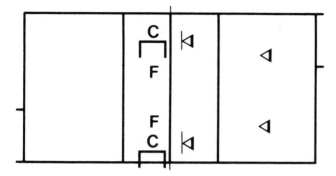

Figure 4-3   *One-on-One Repetitive Blocking*

Equipment and Personnel:
One table, eight balls, a spiker, blocker, feeder, and shagger or shaggers.

DRILL 4-4 BLOCKING DEEP SPIKES

Purpose:
To differentiate between the timing of blocking a close set and a deep set.

Description:
The spiker passes his own ball and the setter places the ball about eight to ten feet from the net. The spiker trys to put the ball on the floor. The blockers wait and jump together without the normal penetration caused by sliding the arms over the net to attack block. On a deep set it is harder for the blockers to time the play so they do not penetrate as much and are in better position to make lateral movements as shown in Photo 4-1.

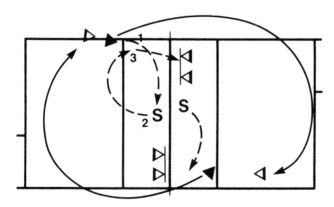

Figure 4-4   *Timing by Depth of Set*

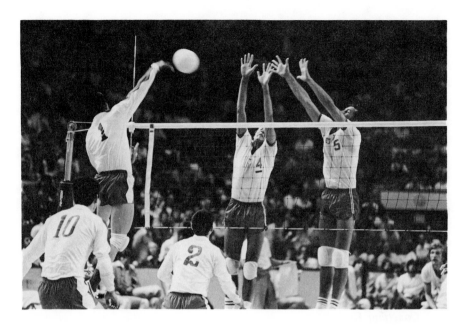

Photo 4-1 *Blocking a Deep Spike. The Polish blockers are taking a lot of vertical surface above the net and have moved the block in to encourage a line shot. The Japanese spiker has opted for a high flat shot toward the middle of the court.* (Credit: Richard Mackson)

Coaching Tip:
On a deep set instruct the end blocker to move toward the center of the court to encourage a line spike and a greater probability of a spiking error.

Equipment and Personnel:
Four balls, four blockers, four spikers, and two setters.

DRILL 4-5 BLOCKING THE RIGHT CROSS

Purpose:
To become familiar with your opponent's offensive plays and to work on your own offense.

Description:
The coach passes to the setter who delivers the ball to any of his attackers. When the right-side attacker or X man moves to the center of the court, the area 2 blocker yells "Cross" and moves over to block the center attacker, leaving the middle blocker free to take the X man. In Photos 4-2 a,b,c, this did *not* occur,

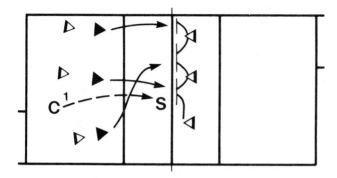

Figure 4-5   *Blocking the Right Cross*

and the middle blocker was isolated against two attackers. The blockers try to get two people blocking at the point of attack by first calling out the offensive play and then trying to react quickly to the set.

Coaching Tip:
The area 2 blocker must get in front of the quick hitter and tell the middle blocker he has him, otherwise the area 2 blocker is a useless spectator.

Equipment and Personnel:
Three blockers, a setter, six to eight spikers, and six balls.

a

Photo 4-2   *The Right Cross. The end blocker does not block No. 11 in Photo 4-2a thus forcing the middle blocker (Photo 4-2b) to jump with him. No. 13 is the X man and is preparing to spike as the middle blocker returns to the floor. Notice that the middle blocker (Photo 4-2c) has not dropped his hands entirely and with a quick extension could be in a position to deflect a low spike.* (Credit: Tom Leja, Event Concepts)

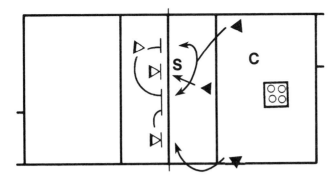

Figure 4-6 *Left Stack versus X or Fake X*

DRILL 4-6 LEFT STACK VERSUS X OR FAKE X

Purpose:
To block the combination hitter on the X or fake X play.

Description:
The middle blocker "commits" or jumps with the quick hitter and if necessary jumps again in the direction of the set without dropping the arms. The stack blocker starts a meter from the net by the left shoulder of the middle blocker. The stack blocker will watch the opponent's right side or combination attacker and either commit and follow that hitter or read and wait for the set, thus being responsible for the playset hitter and all outside sets. Unless the playset (right side

b   c

hitter) gets the majority of the sets it is best for the stack blocker to read and react to the set. Whether the stack blocker commits or reads he should be able to successfully front the playset hitter on the X or fake X play.

Coaching Tip:
The stack blocker should take the first step with the outside foot and then a crossover step with the second step while moving laterally and towards the net.

Equipment and Personnel:
One ballcart, twelve balls, seven players, one coach, and a shagger.

DRILL 4-7 LEFT STACK VERSUS THE FOUR SET

Purpose:
To train the stack blocker to key on the combination hitter and still get up on the four set.

Description:
The stack blocker is in a read assignment and follows the combination hitter in the X route while watching the setter release the ball. If it is an X set the stack blocker is already in front of the combination hitter and is in position to block. The middle blocker commits with the quick hitter and does not expect any help. If there is a four set the stack blocker moves laterally and forms a two person block with the right side player.

Coaching Tips:
Once the stack blocker can make the four set after following the X hitter, call a fake X and then a five for the combination hitter. In a read defense the stack blocker only moves before the set when the combination hitter runs an X

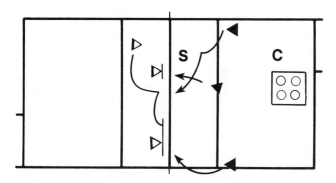

Figure 4-7 *Left Stack versus a Four*

route. When the fake X and five is called for the combination hitter the stack blocker moves after the direction of the set is ascertained so that the stack blocker has further to go against the four set.

Equipment and Personnel:
One ballcart, twelve balls, seven players, one coach, and a shagger.

DRILL 4-8 READING THE PLAY (LEFT BLOCKER)

Purpose:
To teach the left-side blocker he is responsible for *all* sets in zone 4.

Description:
The coach passes balls to the setter in front of the area 4 blocker and two spikers run combination plays at the blocker. The blocker has to keep his hands extended above his head as shown in Photo 4-3 to react immediately to the set. The spiker shags the ball and returns it to the coach. A middle blocker may be added to this drill.

Coaching Tip:
If the player jumps erroneously with the quick attacker, he must keep his arms extended and quickly jump with the second man.

Equipment and Personnel:
One blocker, one setter, and four to six spikers. One ball per spiker.

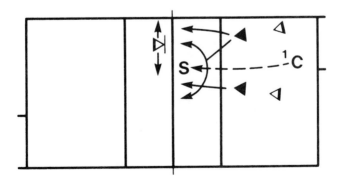

Figure 4-8   *Reading the Play (Left Blocker)*

Photo 4-3   *Area 4 Blocker. Ideally the blocker in this zone should be tall enough to "tiptoe" block the quick hitter with full arm extension and be quick enough to react to the second man running at him.* (Credit: Richard Mackson)

DRILL 4-9 READING THE PLAY (RIGHT BLOCKER)

Purpose:
To teach the right-side blocker he is responsible for *all* sets in zone 2.

Description:
The coach passes balls to the setter who calls plays for two hitters in front of the zone 2 blocker. The blocker has to read the set and key on the right attacker. A middle blocker may be added to this drill.

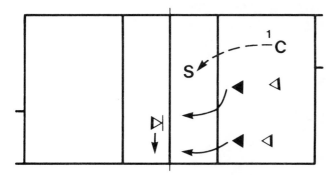

Figure 4-9   *Reading the Play (Right Blocker)*

Coaching Tip:
The end blocker should keep his hand between the ball and the sideline on a close set as shown in Photo 4-4.

Equipment and Personnel:
One or two blockers, one setter, and four to six spikers. One ball per spiker.

DRILL 4-10 RIGHT STACK VERSUS THE COMBINATION HITTER

Purpose:
To stop the combination hitter who starts in area 4.

Description:
The stack blocker starts on the middle or commit blocker's right shoulder. The commit blocker starts in front of the quick hitter favoring the location of his favorite route. The area 4 blocker starts five feet from the sideline. The stack blocker either reads or commits with the combination hitter. In the read defense he stays on the right shoulder of the commit blocker until the set is released and then follows the set to the attacker. Of course, if the combination hitter runs inside the quick hitter and the area 2 hitter is not swinging left, the stack blocker moves with the combination hitter; *but* he still watches the set and then goes to the point of attack in the read defense. In the commit defense the stack blocker follows the combination hitter and jumps with him when the pass is good. On a bad pass the commit is called off and everyone reads; this is signaled by the middle blocker yelling, "Read" in a loud voice.

Photo 4-4   *Area 2 Blocker. A high percentage of balls are set in front of the area 2 blocker. For that reason the player assigned to area 2 should usually be a stronger blocker than the area 4 teammate.* (Credit: Andy Klussmann, Sr.)

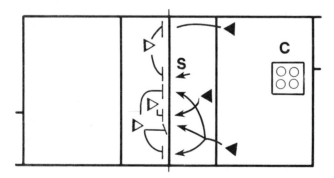

Figure 4-10   *Right Stack versus the Combination Hitter*

Coaching Tip:
This defense is only used when the left side combination hitter is the major threat.

Equipment and Personnel:
One ballcart, twelve balls, and seven players.

DRILL 4-11 RIGHT STACK VERSUS THE FIVE SET

Purpose:
To train the stack blocker to read the setter and make a quick movement to the left sideline.

Description:
The coach tosses the ball to the setter who sets over half of the balls for the right side spiker. The other sets are dispersed equally between the other two spikers. The middle blocker commits on the quick hitter and the other blockers read the set. Although the stack blocker has a long way to go to get to the left sideline he should make every effort to close the seam of the block; even if he has to reach laterally with just the left arm. When the ball is set high the stack blocker should easily reach his assignment.

Coaching Tips:
The commit blocker can jump again on a five set and form a three-person block. The second jump will have to propel the blocker laterally along the net on a low five set in order to quickly close the seam. Remember, if the pass is bad

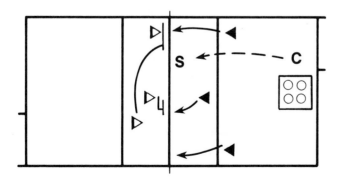

Figure 4-11   *Right Stack versus the Five Set*

and there is no threat of a quick attack, the middle blocker shouts, "Read" and the stack defense is off. The three blockers then use a reading defense with the usual middle blocker switching to the middle from the stack or left side position.

Equipment and Personnel:
One ballcart, twelve balls, seven players, one coach, and a shagger.

DRILL 4-12 BLOCK AND ATTACK

Purpose:
To block and approach to spike after blocking while building endurance.

Description:
The coach stands on a table and spikes balls at the blocker. After blocking, the player immediately backs off the net to spike a ball thrown by another coach or teammate, and the action is quickly repeated.

Coaching Tip:
Vary the sets so that the attacker can increase his range.

Equipment and Personnel:
Four shaggers, two feeders, one coach, one setter, a blocker/attacker, and ten balls are needed for this drill.

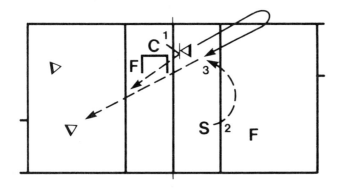

Figure 4-12   *Block and Attack*

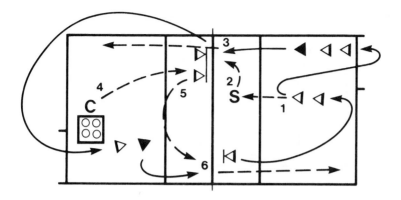

Figure 4-13   *Block and Set*

DRILL 4-13 BLOCK AND SET

Purpose:
To drill blockers to quickly turn to their backcourt and look for the ball after blocking.

Description:
A player in the feeding line passes the ball to the setter who backsets to the spiker who tries to put it away. The blockers try to intercept the spike, but if the ball goes by them the coach throws the ball behind them, simulating an errant dig by a backcourt defender. The closest or fastest blocker then sets the ball to the off blocker who attempts to spike past one blocker, and the drill is repeated. The two blockers stay in their position until the coach tells them to rotate. The other players continually rotate counterclockwise so they spike, shag, put a ball in the cart, dig and spike, block, shag, pass the ball, and spike again to repeat the process.

Coaching Tips:
After blocking, players should pivot on their outside foot and face the center of the court; their legs should be bent so they can quickly dive for the ball.

Equipment and Personnel:
One ballcart, ten balls, one coach, and ten to twelve players.

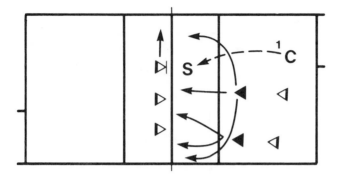

Figure 4-14   *Blocking the Two-Hitter Attack*

Photo 4-5   *Blocking the Setter. A 5-1 setter must be an offensive threat when he is in the front row or the opposition will usually have a two-man block opposing the spikes.* (Credit: Norm Schindler, ASUCLA)

DRILL 4-14 READING THE TWO-HITTER ATTACK

Purpose:

To familiarize the blockers with the offensive threat of a frontcourt setter (see Photo 4-5) and to call out the routes of the two attackers.

Description:

The coach passes the ball to the setter so he has an option of attacking or setting the ball. The setter calls a play before each pass so the spikers will be using different routes to confuse the blockers. The blocker in front of the setter must extend his arms and be prepared to jump with the setter if he is going to attack.

Coaching Tips:

If no attacker is running a route in the area 4 blocker's zone, he will move in front of the setter and be responsible for stopping an attack of the pass. If the area 4 blocker has an attacker in his area, the middle blocker must also be concerned with the setter attacking the pass.

Equipment and Personnel:
Six balls, eight to twelve players, and a coach.

DRILL 4-15 DOUBLE STACK VERSUS TWO HITTERS

Purpose:

To place two blockers in front of the swing hitter while committing one blocker on the quick hitter.

Description:

The setter signals the route to the swing hitter which can include 5's, 4's, X's and fake X's. The quick hitter's assignment can include the A, B, C, slide, flair and 4 or 5 set. The two stack blockers follow the route of the swing attacker and read the setter. On a close pass the stack blocker closest to the setter has to defend against the setter attacking on the second contact.

Coaching Tip:

Teams with good backcourt attackers can send the best backcourt hitter to the opposite side of the swing hitter or to the middle of the court to defeat the double stack. If your opponent has this capability add a backcourt spiker to the attack and have your blockers react to the set.

Equipment and Personnel:

One ballcart, twelve balls, seven to twelve players, one coach, and a shagger.

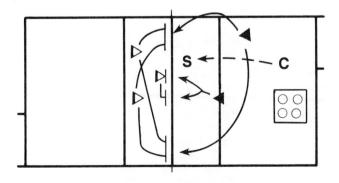

Figure 4-15   *Double Stack versus Two Hitters*

5

Digging

DRILL 5-1 THREE-PERSON PEPPER

Purpose:
To allow the digger to use the court in a game situation by attempting to dig a spike to the setter at the net.

Description:
The spiker stands in area 4 with back to the net and hits to the digger's area of responsibility. The digger directs the spiked ball to the setter who jump-sets the ball to the spiker; the action is repeated until the ball hits the floor. Any of the three players can initiate the sequence.

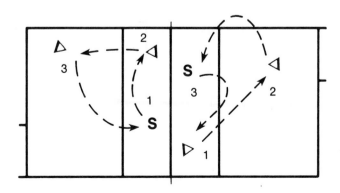

Figure 5-1 *Three-Person Pepper*

Coaching Tips:

If the beginning spiker cannot control the spike the set may be caught and tossed and hit. We insist that the setter jumpset all good digs within the three meter line. Jumpsets give the block less time to react and on many occasions take a blocker out of the play.

Equipment and Personnel:

One ball to every three players. If there are not enough courts the setter and spiker can stand against the wall to simulate a net.

DRILL 5-2 TWO-PERSON PEPPER

Purpose:

To give the entire team an opportunity to dig and set using many repetitions in a short period of time. This drill is usually used in the beginning of a practice or pre-match warm-up.

Description:

Two players team up with one ball and stand about 20 feet apart. A team of twelve could place six players on each side of the net. Player A spikes to Player B who digs back to A. Player A sets to B who spikes to A, and the players continue to spike, dig, and set to each other.

Coaching Tips:

The players should vary the placement of hard spikes and off-speed shots so that the defender has to go to the floor to retrieve the shots as in Photo 5-1. Some coaches prefer that one of the partners start with her back to the net and spike all the balls at her partner, then change places. The reason for this placement is to simulate game conditions so that the digger will control the ball on her side of the net.

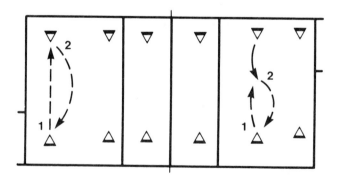

Figure 5-2 *Pepper*

Photo 5-1   *The Sprawl. This technique is the most frequently used method of retrieving low balls. The player uses the forearm pass to control the ball and slides forward on her arms as her body extends along the floor absorbing the shock. This technique requires little arm and shoulder strength.* (Credit: Norm Schindler, ASUCLA)

Equipment and Personnel:
One ball to every two players; the entire squad may participate in this drill at the same time.

DRILL 5-3 DOUBLES

Purpose:
To stimulate movement and promote "quick feet."

Description:
The coach stands on the sideline near the net and passes the ball to either of two attackers on his side of the court; this pass counts as the first of three contacts. The player receiving the pass must set the ball to his teammate who attempts to put it away. If successful, the players rotate to the end of the line; if the defenders put the ball away, the attackers become the defenders. If the defenders lose to three attackers in a row, they are penalized and must perform ten quick dives before the coach resumes the drill. The two defenders stay in until they beat the attackers.

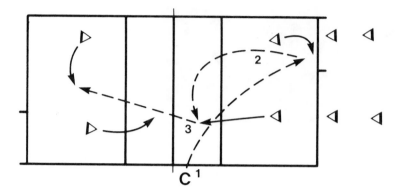

Figure 5-3   *Doubles*

Coaching Tip:
When the defenders are too weak or unskilled to dive, substitute sprawls, rolls, or push-ups for the penalty.

Equipment and Personnel:
Three balls, six to twelve players, and a coach.

DRILL 5-4 DIG AND SPIKE

Purpose:
To train the area 4 spiker to dig and quickly approach to spike.

Description:
The coach stands on a table and spikes at the area 4 player who digs the ball to the setter who is positioned near the net between areas 2 and 3. After the dig the spiker swings toward the sideline for a wide set and tries to defeat two blockers. This is repeated for ten trials; then the player rests for ten trials and repeats the drill. Use up to three repetitions depending on the condition of the players.

Coaching Tip:
Use some dinks to area 3 to cause the spiker to dive and then hurry to his feet to run back to area 4 to spike. After a dive the setter may have to set higher than usual to give the player time to reach his assignment.

Equipment and Personnel:
One table, six balls, one coach, one setter, two blockers, a spiker and three to six shaggers.

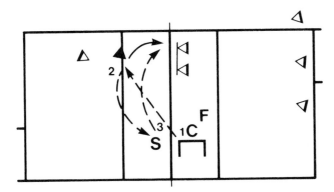

Figure 5-4   *Dig and Spike*

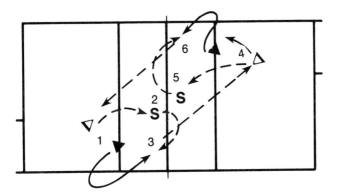

Figure 5-5   *Area 1 and 2 Digging*

DRILL 5-5 AREA 1 AND 2 DIGGING

Purpose:
To teach the spiker to get quickly into the assigned digging position after attacking and to approach quickly for the attack after digging. This drill is more advanced than the previous drill because the players must have very good ball control skills.

Description:
Two diggers line up on each side of the court in area 1 and 2. The digger in area 2 transitions between attacking and digging by the three meter line. The digger in area 1 digs and backs up the attacker and then returns to the digging position. A setter on each side of the net delivers the set according to the verbal calls of the area 2 hitters. They call ''Five'' for a high set and ''Quick'' for a lower

set. The hitters attack the ball at two-thirds speed and only hit to area 1 or 2. At the college level the drill can continue for several minutes before the ball hits the court. This drill is not recommended for teams with poor ball control.

Coaching Tips:
Make sure the digger in area 1 follows the attacker to the net and stops in a low position to simulate recovering a blocked ball. Watch all diggers to make sure they are in the proper position when the ball is attacked.

Equipment and Personnel:
Four diggers, two setters, and a ball.

DRILL 5-6 AREA 4 DIGGING

Purpose:
To teach the left side spiker to quickly get away from the net after spiking and establish a defensive position at the three meter line.

Description:
The ball is served to the left front spiker who can receive in either area 4 or 5. The player passes to the setter and spikes an outside set to the digger in area 4. The digger then receives an outside set and spikes to area 4 and the action is repeated. When the ball hits the floor the action is restarted by the server putting another ball into play.

Coaching Tips:
This drill is for varsity athletes who can hit control spikes to each other. This is usually a two-thirds speed hit but can be faster with better diggers.

Equipment and Personnel:
One server, two spikers, two setters, a ballcart, and ten balls.

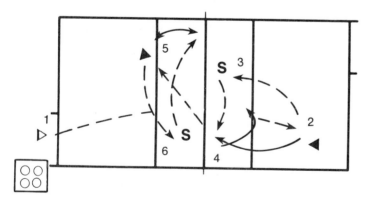

Figure 5-6   *Area 4 Digging*

DRILL 5-7 BACKCOURT DIGGING—NO BLOCK

Purpose:
To practice digging balls that are set off the net.

Description:
The coach stands near the attack line in the center of the court and alternates throwing sets to area 2 and 4 spikers. The defenders try to dig to the two frontcourt shaggers. The shaggers have their backs to the spikers and are watching to prevent any balls from rolling under the spikers' feet. Four spikers alternate hitting in this fastpaced drill.

Coaching Tips:
The depth of the set will depend on the ability of the spikers. When working with advanced players, the sets will be ten feet from the net so the diggers will have a chance to touch every ball. When the hitters are small or poorly skilled, the sets can be placed very close to the net.

Equipment and Personnel:
Ten balls, a ballcart, a feeder, coach, three diggers, four spikers, and four shaggers.

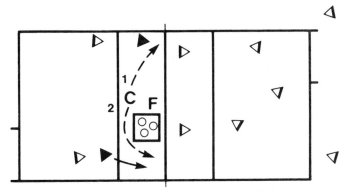

Figure 5-7 *Backcourt Digging – No Block*

Photo 5-2 *Backcourt Digging. When conditions prevent the spiker from hitting a powerful shot, the blockers should stay down and let the backcourt defenders have an unobstructed view of the ball. This will allow them to get in position for the dig.* (Credit: Norm Schindler, ASUCLA)

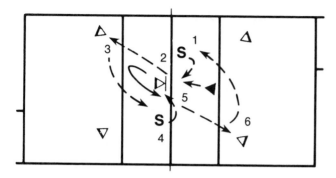

Figure 5-8   *Digging the Quick Hitter*

DRILL 5-8 DIGGING THE QUICK HITTER

Purpose:
To teach the area 1 and 5 diggers to dig the spike of a quick set from area 3 of the opponent's court.

Description:
The spiker hits a quick set (1) in the center third of the court opposed by one blocker who has been instructed to zone block to prevent the spiker from going into area 6. To avoid the blocker the spiker must hit the ball into area 1 or 5 where the defenders are waiting. The spiker hits the ball (2) at two-thirds speed so the diggers can direct the ball (3) to their setter who delivers a set (4) to their middle attacker who hits (5) to the defender who digs (6) to the setter. This action is repeated until the ball hits the floor whereupon it is put into play by one of the diggers.

Coaching Tips:
Instruct the spikers to try and hit the ball with less than their maximum effort so that it may stay in play. The diggers must transition between backing up their spiker and getting into their defensive position.

Equipment and Personnel:
One ball, four diggers, two setters, and two attackers. Extra players can shag until the coach works them on the drill.

DRILL 5-9 QUICK TO HIGH SET ADJUSTMENT

Purpose:
To train the defenders to move from their starting defensive position deeper into their court to dig spikes from the outside attackers.

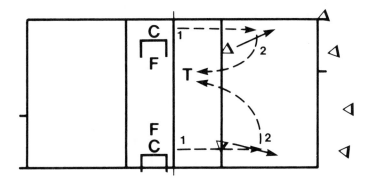

Figure 5-9   *Quick to High Set Adjustment*

Description:
The area 1 and 5 defenders start on the attack line so that they can retrieve an errant pass, dig the quick hitter, or field a ball the setter dumps over the net. The coach yells "Outside" to indicate a wide set and the defenders quickly move to within ten feet of the endline to dig a spike from the coach. This drill can be run with one of two coaches standing on tables in areas 2 and 4. When using one coach, alternate spiking to each digging line. The digger can stay in for several repetitions or rotate with the shaggers after every dig. A target player retrieves balls from both digging lines and gives them to the feeders.

Coaching Tip:
Start the defenders fifteen feet from the net (instead of ten feet) if your opponents' quick attackers cannot spike the ball into the frontcourt.

Equipment and Personnel:
Two tables, twelve balls, two coaches, two feeders, one target player, two diggers, and four to seven shaggers.

DRILL 5-10 LATERAL MOVEMENT

Purpose:
To train the middle back defender to move laterally.

Description:
The coach stands on a table and spikes off the top of two blockers. The digger stands on the endline and reacts to the spike as it ricochets off the blockers. After ten trials the digger rests while his partner drills; the drill is repeated until each player has thirty digs.

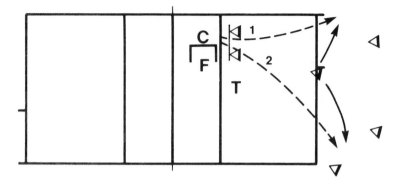

Figure 5-10   *Lateral Movement*

Photo 5-3   *Middle Back Defender. The defender in the middle back has to move laterally to dig balls hit off the blockers.* (Credit: Norm Schindler, ASUCLA)

Coaching Tip:

The emphasis should be on digging the ball high so that someone can run under it even when it is off the court.

Equipment and Personnel:

A table, coach, feeder, target player, two blockers, one digger, and three to seven players to dig and shag.

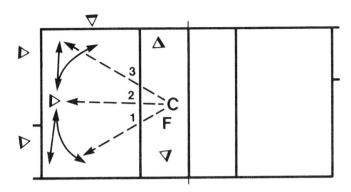

Figure 5-11   *The Pit*

DRILL 5-11 THE PIT

Purpose:
To place a player in a defensive position and test him to the limit of his defensive capabilities.

Description:
The digger is surrounded by his peers who have just gone through or will go through the drill. The coach hits balls near the player in a rapid fashion causing him to dive, roll, sprawl, and grovel to dig everything he can. The object is to condition the player to attempt to dig every ball; not to make judgments, but to react quickly. The player's teammates shag and encourage the digger.

Photo 5-4   *Go for It. Better players go for every ball and often make saves that average players deem impossible.* (Credit: Steve Harris)

Coaching Tip:

To extend the player's range, alternate spiking balls just out of his range interspersed with balls he can reach.

Equipment and Personnel:

Twelve balls and six to twelve players.

DRILL 5-12 PURSUIT

Purpose:

To extend the effective range of the entire defense.

Description:

The coach stands on a table and spikes a high flat ball off the blockers so that it travels out of bounds. The players pursue the ball so that the digger can pass the ball to someone close by rather than trying to pass the ball 30 feet to his nearest teammate.

Coaching Tips:

To avoid injuries, do not allow play on adjoining courts when using this drill. Players should try to set the ball to the frontcourt and score.

Equipment and Personnel:

One table, six balls, two blockers, and six defenders.

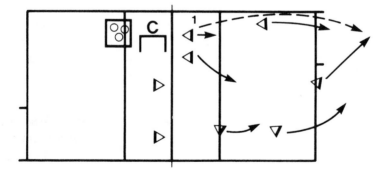

Figure 5-12   *Pursuit*

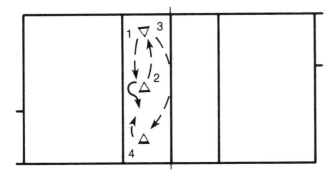

Figure 5-13 *Overhand Pass Drill*

DRILL 5-13 OVERHAND PASS DRILL

Purpose:
To teach the players to take a ball traveling at a slow speed with their hands. A ball that is passed slowly over the net is called a free ball. Free balls should be passed quickly and accurately so the setter can beat the blockers with a quick set.

Description:
Two players stand near the sideline with one player in the middle. The player in the middle passes the ball back to the player on the sideline using a low quick trajectory. The ball then travels to the other sideline as the player in the center turns 180 degrees to receive a pass from the other direction. The players on the sideline also use their hands to pass the ball.

Coaching Tip:
Have the player in the center collapse to the floor as the ball is being passed. This collapse pass technique is particularly effective in passing low balls that would otherwise have to be passed by the forearms. The player collapsing lowers the center of gravity by bending the knees and first contacting the floor with the buttocks and then lower back before swinging the legs forward to regain a standing position. We believe our overhand passes are faster and more accurate using the collapse method.

Equipment and Personnel:
One ball for every three players. Up to six groups of three players can participate on one court.

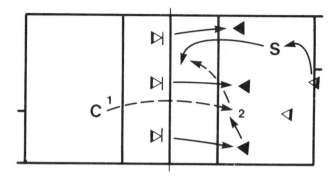

Figure 5-14   *Free Ball Pass*

DRILL 5-14 FREE BALL PASS

Purpose:
To improve the accuracy of the free ball pass and the free ball play.

Description:
The coach stands behind three blockers and yells "Free" whereupon the defenders move into their serve-reception formation and prepare to run their free ball play.

Coaching Tips:
Have the first team practice as a unit and work the key substitutes in.

Equipment and Personnel:
Three balls, nine players, and a coach.

DRILL 5-15 DOWN BLOCK

Purpose:
To train the backcourt defenders to cover more court on a down block.

Description:
The coach stands on a table and yells "Down" whereupon the middle back player moves into the court as the area 1 and 5 defenders move back. The players react to the ball and try to score against a two-person block.

Photo 5-5   *Free Ball. The digger has called for the ball and prepares to use the forearm pass.* (Credit: Norm Schindler, ASUCLA)

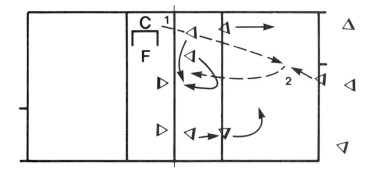

Figure 5-15   *Down Block*

Photo 5-6   *Down Ball. The backcourt defender alertly dives to dig an off-speed shot to the frontcourt after the blockers stayed down on the play.* (Credit: Norm Schindler, ASUCLA)

Coaching Tip:

The defenders should not be moving their feet when the coach contacts the ball. When they are stopped and facing the attacker, they can react in any direction.

Equipment and Personnel:

One table, one coach, and eight to twelve players.

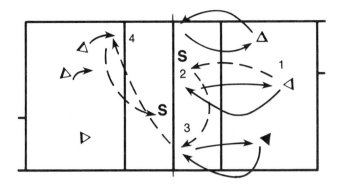

Figure 5-16   *Pepper Over the Net*

DRILL 5-16 PEPPER OVER THE NET

Purpose:
To read the attacker and get into the right defensive area.

Description:
Three spiker diggers are on each side of the net along with a setter. The spikers hit at two-thirds speed so the ball will be kept in play. The players keep transitioning between attacking and digging.

Coaching Tips:
The diggers watch the pass to the setter, the direction of the set, and the attackers' approach. They move to the area where they think the ball will go (staying within their area of responsibility) and stop just prior to the attacker contacting the ball.

Equipment and Personnel:
Eight players and a ball.

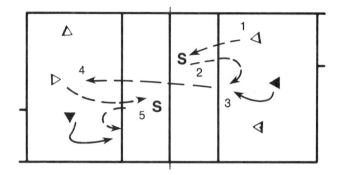

Figure 5-17   *Digging Backcourt Hits*

DRILL 5-17 DIGGING BACKCOURT HITS

Purpose:
To practice digging attacks of backcourt players that are a basic offensive tactic of the 5-1 defense.

Description:
Three players on each side of the net are assigned defensive positions and hit sets by taking off behind the three meter line. The players on the other side of the net dig the ball to their setter and call for the set and attempt to put the ball away. The coach stands at the net and lets the spiker know when he has landed on or over the line before taking off to spike.

Coaching Tip:
Make sure that the area 1 and 5 diggers' outside foot is forward so that the dig will more likely be controlled into the center of the court.

Equipment and Personnel:
One ball, six players, and a coach.

6

Side-Outs

DRILL 6-1 OUTSIDE HITTER VERSUS MIDDLE BACK DEFENSE

Purpose:
To defeat the right back defender in the middle back defense.

Description:
The hitters form one spiking line in area 4 and either loop a dink over the middle blocker as shown in Photo 6-1 or hit a high flat shot over the end blocker. After the spike, the hitter blocks while the defense tries to score.

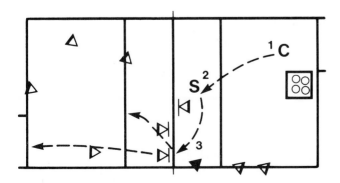

Figure 6-1 *Outside Hitter versus Middle Back Defense*

Photo 6-1   *Dinking over the Middle Blocker. Tim Hovland (No. 10) releases a dink shot over UCLA's two-man block; a very effective maneuver for a powerful spiker.* (Credit: Norm Schindler, ASUCLA)

Coaching Tip:
Watch the spiker to make sure he uses the same approach for the dink and the high flat shot. The tendency is for the attacker to use a slow approach for the dink.

Equipment and Personnel:
Six balls, one ballcart, one coach, and ten to twelve players.

DRILL 6-2 OUTSIDE HITTER VERSUS MIDDLE IN DEFENSE

Purpose:
To spike over the middle blocker with a high flat shot.

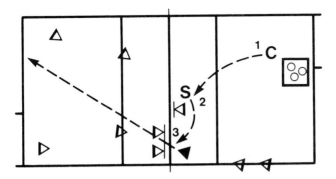

Figure 6-2   *Outside Hitter versus Middle in Defense*

Photo 6-2 *Hitting the Fingers. Peter Ehrman is a 5 ft. 10 in. spiker who had to learn the high flat shot when confronted with taller blockers.* (Credit: Norm Schindler, ASUCLA)

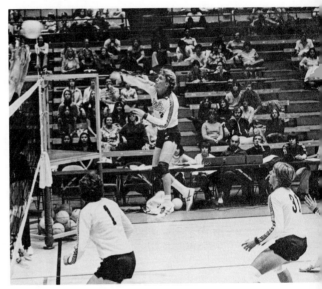

Description:

The spiker hits the middle blocker's fingers (see Photo 6-2) so the spike travels into the undefended area of the backcourt or beyond. The defense tries to score and the setter, spiker, and middle blocker oppose them if there is a rally.

Coaching Tip:

The spike must travel horizontally or slightly upward when the spiker is confronted with a big middle blocker.

Equipment and Personnel:

Six balls, a ballcart, one coach, and nine to twelve players.

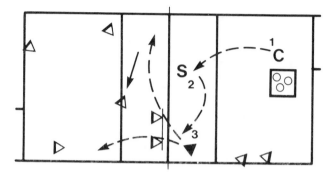

Figure 6-3   *Outside Hitter versus Off-Blocker Defense*

DRILL 6-3 OUTSIDE HITTER VERSUS OFF-BLOCKER DEFENSE

Purpose:
To direct off-speed shots to open areas of the court.

Description:
The spikers form a line in area 4 or 2 and attempt to hit an off-speed shot to the area vacated by the off-blocker whose responsibility in this defense is the area behind the other two blockers. Another vulnerable area is an off-speed shot that lands within a foot or two of the sideline.

Coaching Tip:
These two off-speed shots are for advanced players who have already mastered the various spikes. In competition the novice and intermediate player would have better percentages hitting away.

Equipment and Personnel:
Six balls, a ballcart, one coach, and nine to twelve players.

DRILL 6-4 QUICK HITTER AUDIBILIZING

Purpose:
To give the quick hitter practice in calling for a set after the pass.

Description:
The ball is served anywhere on the court to either of two passers and the hitter calls for a C, slide, A, B, or flair and uses the proper approach to reach the set. Refer to the beginning of Chapter Three for the proper approach for those sets.

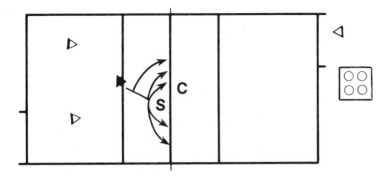

Figure 6-4   *Quick Hitter Audibilizing*

Coaching Tip:

The coach stands on the side of the net in the center of the court in the middle blocking position and encourages the hitter to call for a set that gives him some distance from the middle blocker. The proper call depends on the location of the pass since the quick hitter runs to the setter.

Equipment and Personnel:

Two passers, one server, one setter, one attacker, a cart full of balls, and a coach. If necessary up to five passers can be used to insure accuracy.

DRILL 6-5 SPLIT HITTERS

Purpose:

To set the ball to either outside spiker with a trajectory and delivery that will beat the middle blocker. The set to area 4 is commonly known as a four set and the backset as a five set.

Description:

The coach passes a good ball to the setter and he delivers a set that is low and fast enough to keep the middle blocker (No. 13 in Photo 6-3) out of the play. The middle blocker tries to read the setter and get to the attacker before the ball does. After the spiker hits, he shags the ball and runs it to the ballcart next to the coach. The blockers try to score by stuffing the ball or deflecting it to a teammate who sets to one of the other two defenders.

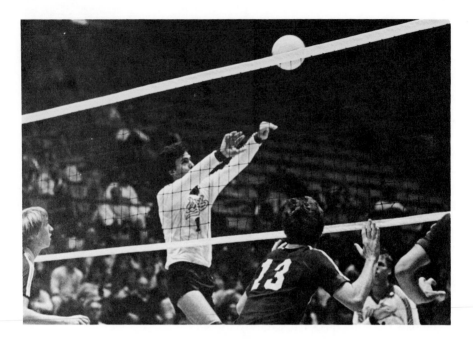

Photo 6-3   *The Shoot Set. This low fast four set can only be delivered to a coordinated spiker with good quickness. It will always give him a one-on-one attack situation.* (Credit: Norm Schindler, ASUCLA)

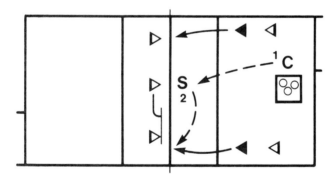

Figure 6-5   *Split Hitters*

Coaching Tips:

Some slower players must be set higher than their quicker teammates; the coach should point out these individual differences to the setter. Keep the three blockers working together for three to five minutes.

Equipment and Personnel:

Eight balls, a ballcart, one coach, and seven to twelve players.

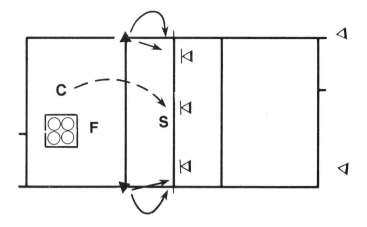

Figure 6-6   *Split Hitters with Audibles*

DRILL 6-6 SPLIT HITTERS WITH AUDIBLES

Purpose:
To beat the middle blocker by calling for low fast sets to the antenna. See Photo 6-3 for an example of this type of set.

Description:
The coach tosses good balls to the setter about 80% of the time. When the attackers see a good toss they call for a fast set for the antenna. The right side attacker can yell "Quick" and the left attacker "Shoot". The setter should jump set every good pass to hold the middle blocker; if the middle blocker does not stay with the setter, the setter should attack the ball. The sets should be fast enough to make the middle blocker late and leave a hole between the blockers. When the coach tosses the ball around the three meter line, the spikers will receive a higher set and will have two blockers to contend with.

Coaching Tip:
The setter must be a threat to attack the ball and *must* jumpset every good toss or the middle blocker will get to the outside hitters.

Equipment and Personnel:
A ballcart with ten balls, two shaggers, a feeder, one coach, a setter, two hitters, and three blockers.

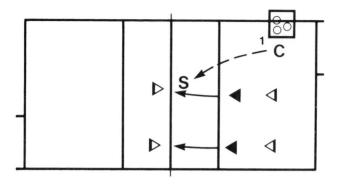

Figure 6-7   *Stack Left*

DRILL 6-7 STACK LEFT

Purpose:
To concentrate on attacking in areas 3 and 4 with a simple play.

Description:
The coach varies his passes along the net, and the setter delivers the A set (as shown in Photo 6-4) or a four set. The spikers continue approaching until they receive the set, then they shag the ball and return it to the cart.

Coaching Tip:
The spiker should take off well in front of the net as shown in Photo 6-4 so that she can take a full armswing.

Equipment and Personnel:
Six balls, one ballcart, one coach, and seven to twelve players.

DRILL 6-8 STACK LEFT WITH AUDIBLES

Purpose:
To defeat the block with two hitters who call for an audible depending on the location of the pass.

Description:
On a good pass, the outside hitter hits a fast set we call a "Shoot" which is designed to beat the center blocker. If the pass is poor the outside hitter calls for a "Four" which is a higher set. The quick attacker calls for a "C," "Slide,"

Photo 6-4   *The A Set. This high fast set should be delivered to a good attacker even when one blocker is keying against her.* (Credit: Norm Schindler, ASUCLA)

"A," "B," "Flair," or a "quick set" depending on the location of the pass in re-lation to the middle blocker. The object is to use a route to distance the middle blocker from the point of attack. The servers serve anywhere on the court and retrieve the balls between serves. The passers try to pass low and fast to the setter who stands ten feet from the right sideline at the net. The setter listens for the audibles and chooses the set which will put the attacker on a one-on-one situation when the pass is accurate. On a bad pass the setter will set a four. The setter will jumpset the ball on every good pass and will attack the pass when the block is not defending against that tactic.

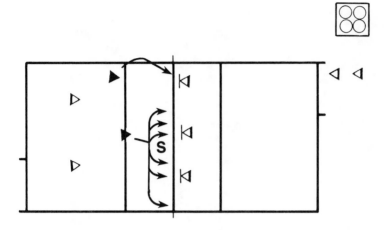

Figure 6-8   *Stack Left with Audibles*

Coaching Tip:
Give the attackers immediate feedback on the selection of their audible in relation to the pass.

Equipment and Personnel:
A ballcart with ten balls, two servers, three blockers, two attackers, two passers, and a setter.

DRILL 6-9 PLAY C-4

Purpose:
To put pressure on the area 2 blocker by running two attackers into his area.

Description:
The quick spiker runs six to eight feet from the setter as shown in Photo 6-5, and the area 4 spiker approaches for a quick four set. This drill is started with a serve, and the two spikers are opposed by two blockers. The server plays middle back defense after serving, and the three defenders play it out against the four players siding out. Two extra spikers rotate in from the sidelines.

Coaching Tip:
The area 3 spiker hits every set he can reach and does not let anything go, even if he thinks it is for the area 4 spiker.

Equipment and Personnel:
Six balls, one ballcart, and nine to twelve players.

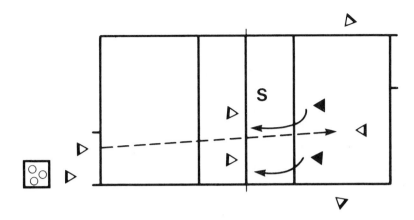

Figure 6-9 *Play 4 C*

Photo 6-5 *The C Set. The spiker (No. 30) used the same timing for the takeoff for the C set as he did for an A set; that is, he is in the air as the setter is releasing the ball.* (Credit: Norm Schindler.)

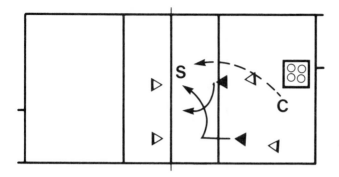

Figure 6-10 *Tandem*

DRILL 6-10 TANDEM

Purpose:
To emphasize to the area 4 spiker to wait until the middle blocker moves to key on the quick hitter before approaching toward the setter.

Description:
The setter signals for the tandem. The area 4 spiker runs straight for the net and then breaks inside. The coach varies the passes from different areas of the court.

Coaching Tip:
Setters have a tendency to drop their hands when delivering the C set which tips off an observant middle blocker and gives him an extra step. The coach must watch to make sure the hands are kept at approximately the same height for all sets.

Equipment and Personnel:
Six balls, one ballcart, one coach, and seven to twelve players.

DRILL 6-11 STACK RIGHT

Purpose:
To concentrate on attacking in areas 2 and 3 with a simple play.

Description:
Two blockers face an area 2 and an area 3 spiker. The area 2 spiker runs in for a five set as shown in Photos 6-6 a, b, c while the area 3 spiker jumps for a quick set (see Photo 6-6b). The coach passes the ball to various locations along the net, and the setter delivers the ball to either attacker. The attacker does not rotate until he has been set, and then he shags the ball and returns it to the cart.

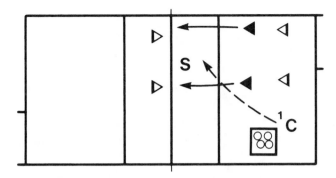

Figure 6-11 *Stack Right*

Coaching Tips:
When the ball is passed to the center of the court, the five set will almost always give the spiker a one-on-one attack situation. Add a third blocker to make the team siding out work harder and instruct the setter to jam the pass.

Equipment and Personnel:
Six balls, one ballcart, one coach, and six to twelve players.

Photo 6-6 *The Five Set. Even when the quick hitter (No. 1 in Photo 6-6a) is late, the five set will usually prevent a good two-man block from forming, as evidenced by the hole in the block left by the Japanese in Photo 6-6c.* (Credit: Norm Schindler, ASUCLA)

b   c

DRILL 6-12 PLAY C 5

Purpose:
To confuse the middle blocker.

Description:
The area 3 spiker runs and takes off about eight feet from the setter in anticipation of a fast set (called a C) that will catch the opposition with their block down as shown in Photo 6-7. When the middle blocker starts moving with the area 3 attacker, the backset to the sideline is used (five set) to create a one-on-one situation. The coach passes to the setter who delivers a C or five set; the hitters stay in until they are set, then shag the ball and return it to the ballcart. The blockers stay together as a unit for three to five minutes.

Coaching Tips:
The quick hitter should cut back to area 1 to avoid the stronger middle blocker. The setter should jumpset every ball he can and jam when a blocker does not oppose him.

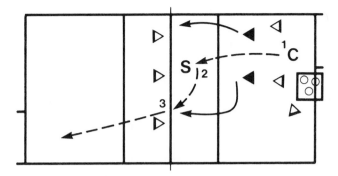

Figure 6-12 *Play C 5*

Photo 6-7 *The Height of the C Set. The setter should deliver this ball as high as the spiker can reach. This tactic makes the blockers jump as high as they can when the quick hitter takes off and opens up the attack for other players. Doug Partie (No. 20) is preparing to spike a set over three feet above the net.* (Credit: Norm Schindler, ASUCLA)

Equipment and Personnel:
Six balls, a ballcart, a coach, and nine to twelve players.

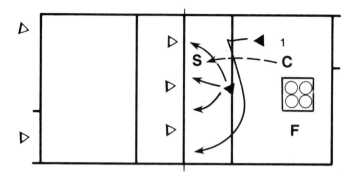

Figure 6-13   *Swing Hitter*

DRILL 6-13 SWING HITTER

Purpose:
To match up the outside hitter against the weakest end blocker.

Description:
The outside or swing hitter receives a signal from the setter to hit a four set and the quick hitter is free to audibilize after watching the pass from the coach. The swing hitter takes a step or two straight at the area 2 blocker before swinging to the left side to hit a four set. This play would be called in competition when the area 2 blocker is weaker than the area 4 blocker. Not all players have the agility to be a swing hitter. This tactic is now used by many college teams after being popularized by our 1984 Men's Olympic Team.

Coaching Tip:
If the swing hitter is a good passer, let him receive the serve in area 1 to initiate the drill. The depth will give him an easier route to the other side of the court.

Equipment and Personnel:
Twelve balls, a ballcart, nine or more players, and a coach.

DRILL 6-14 BACKCOURT SPIKER

Purpose:
To add variety to the attack and to enable the setter to deliver the ball to a hot spiker when they rotate to the backcourt.

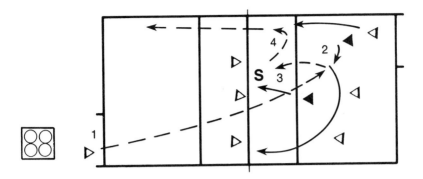

Figure 6-14   *Backcourt Spikers*

Description:
Place the side out team in one of their three two-hitter formations and have the setter signal the backcourt spiker to go to the open area of the court. The best percentage backcourt attacks come from the right sideline (D sets) or the center of the court (pipe set). The backcourt players can call for a D or pipe anytime but we have the setter signal the play for sideouts. The D and pipe sets should be delivered about five to eight feet from the net depending on the broad jumping capabilities of the attacker. Use the full side out team on this drill so all the players see the signals and get out of the attacker's way. This drill can be run against a server and three blockers or a full defense.

Coaching Tip:
If the setter jumpsets and occasionally attacks the pass it takes out the blocker who is responsible for the D set.

Equipment and Personnel:
Twelve balls, a ballcart, and ten to twelve players.

DRILL 6-15 FRONTCOURT PASS

Purpose:
To serve frontcourt players to familiarize them with this tactic.

Description:
A player serves to area 2, 3, or 4, and the attackers run play 1 which is a four set to area 4; an A set to area 3; and a five set to area 2. The blockers attempt to stuff the spike, and the attackers rotate when they have been set.

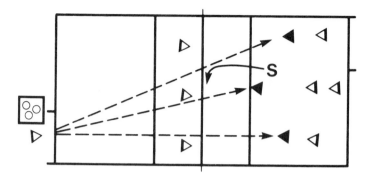

Figure 6-15   *Front Court Pass*

Photo 6-8   *Frontcourt Passer. The timing of a play is different when the ball is passed from the frontcourt. The passer should concentrate on locking the elbows and raising them horizontally to the floor as Karch Kiraly so aptly demonstrates here.* (Credit: Norm Schindler, ASUCLA)

Coaching Tip:
The player who passes the ball must make sure he is concentrating fully on the pass and not moving his feet to start his approach.

Equipment and Personnel:
Eight balls, a ballcart, one server, three blockers, and four to eight players.

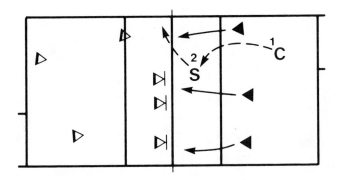

Figure 6-16   *Setter Dumps*

DRILL 6-16 SETTER DUMPS

Purpose:
To provide deception in the attack.

Description:
The setter has the option of setting a four, A, or five set or dumping the ball. A backcourt player while forward of the attack line must contact the ball when at least part of it is below the level of the top of the net; for this reason setters penetrating from the *backcourt* should not jump when dumping the ball. Of course, a *frontcourt* setter should jump and jam the ball sharply downward.

Coaching Tip:
Since the ball delivered by a backcourt setter will stay in the air a long time (because of a flat trajectory), it must be directed toward a definite weakness in the opponents' defense.

Equipment and Personnel:
Six defenders, three attackers, a setter, and coach.

a

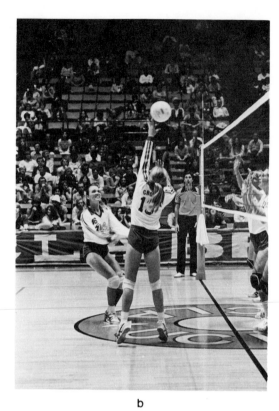

b

Photo 6-9 *A Dump Shot by Backcourt Setter. In Photo 6-9a the setter raises both hands as if to set; in b she extends her body and left arm and quickly tips the ball toward the net. In Photo 6-9c the blockers watch the ball sail over their heads.* (Credit: Norm Schindler, ASUCLA)

c

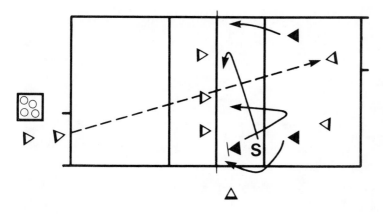

Figure 6-17 *Quick Attacker in Left Front*

DRILL 6-17 QUICK ATTACKER
IN THE LEFT FRONT

Purpose:
To run an effective side-out when the quick hitter is in the left front.

Description:
The server directs the ball to area 1 or 2 which is the usual place opponents serve to when the setter also starts in area 4. After the serve, the server plays middle back, another server stands ready so there is no "dead" time between serves. The receiving team is in its starting lineup and will use a quick-hitter substitute every five hits to give the starter and first substitute timing with the setter. Halfway through the drill the front row flip-flops with the back if the two-setter system is used. The four defenders try to score versus the first team trying to side-out.

Coaching Tip:
Since the emphasis here is on siding out, do not use a full defense or there will be fewer opportunities to run the play in the specified time allotted.

Equipment and Personnel:
Six balls, one ballcart, and twelve players.

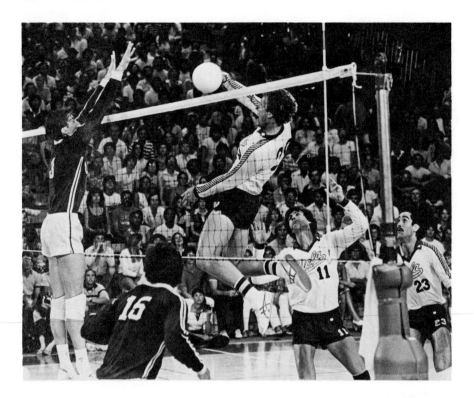

Photo 6-10 *Bad Pass. Any time the ball is passed into area 4 the quick hitter approaches for an A set since he no longer can run 6–8 feet from the left sideline for a C set. Steve Salmons is shown cutting back on an A set over the area 4 blocker who is caught waiting for No. 23 to hit a four set.* (Credit: Norm Schindler, ASUCLA)

DRILL 6-18 RIGHT X

Purpose:
To perfect the classic play in volleyball (for a team that can pass well).

Description:
Two servers and three blockers oppose the offense who is only allowed to run the right X. The server serves to the X hitter most of the time to complicate his route and then plays middle back. The emphasis is on the first side-out play so there are no defenders in areas 1 and 5 to cut down the chance of rallies. If the defense digs, then the defense tries to score. When the ball hits the floor, the next server quickly serves to teach the offense to be prepared even if the referee blows a quick whistle.

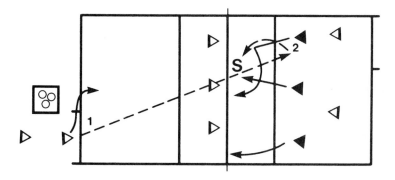

Figure 6-18   *Right X*

Photo 6-11   *Right X. The quick hitter (No. 14) at UCLA is instructed to spike every set he can reach; if he cannot reach the ball, the X man will. (Credit: Norm Schindler, ASUCLA)*

Coaching Tips:

The X spiker should be on his second step (left foot) as the setter touches the ball (see Photo 6-11a). His third step (Photo 6-11b) places him directly behind the quicker hitter (No. 14) so both attackers are in front of the middle blocker.

Equipment and Personnel:

Eight balls, a ballcart, and eleven to twelve spikers.

Coaching Tip:

The player who passes the ball must make sure he is concentrating fully on the pass and not moving his feet to start his approach.

Equipment and Personnel:

Eight balls, a ballcart, one server, three blockers, and four to eight players.

DRILL 6-19 FAKE X

Purpose:

To introduce the Fake X.

Description:

The coach passes the ball to the setter, and the area 2 and 3 hitters run a fake-X pattern as shown in Photos 6-12 a, b. The hitters are opposed by two blockers who work together for three to five minutes. The spiker who hits the ball shags and puts the ball in the cart and waits in the spiking line.

Coaching Tip:

The spiker running the fake-X route must come behind the setter to disguise his route.

Equipment and Personnel:

Eight balls, a ballcart, coach, and seven to twelve players.

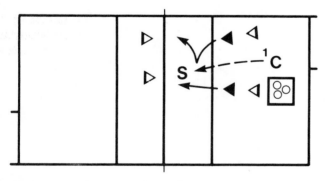

Figure 6-19   *Fake X (No Left Attacker)*

Photo 6-12   *Fake-X. The Fake-X set is shown in Photo 6-12b; it is a set that will be spiked over the opposing middle blocker as he is returning to the floor.* (Credit: Norm Schindler, ASUCLA)

DRILL 6-20 X OR FAKE X

Purpose:
To confuse the block.

Description:
The setter puts up two fingers for an X and three fingers for a fake X. She conceals the signals from the blockers. The area 2 spiker runs both routes the same way until the third step: 1) she steps with the right foot toward the setter; 2) she steps with the left foot behind the setter; and 3) for the X she continues

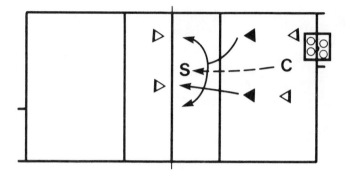

Figure 6-20 *X or Fake X (No Left Attacker)*

by the setter or for the fake she pushes off the left foot to the sideline; 4) the fourth step is with the left, and when that is taken the player leaves the floor with a two-foot takeoff.

Coaching Tip:
Do not introduce the ball until the players have mastered the four-step approach as shown in Photo 6-13.

Equipment and Personnel:
Eight balls, a ballcart, a coach, and seven to twelve players.

a   b

Photo 6-13 *Four-Step Approach. In Photo 6-13a Patty Orozco Dodd is already completing her first step; in b she is on her second step with her left foot; in c she is about to land on her right foot for her third step; in d she is landing on her left foot for her fourth and last step as she prepares to take off; in e she is pushing off by forcibly contracting her ankles as her arms are swinging above her shoulders; and in f she is preparing to hit the ball.* (Credit: Norm Schindler, ASUCLA)

c

d

e

f

Photo 6-13

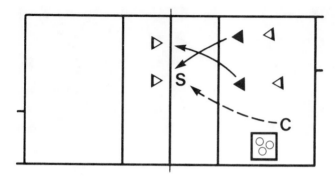

Figure 6-21   *Reverse X*

DRILL 6-21 REVERSE X

Purpose:
To switch the hitting assignments of the area 2 and 3 spikers. This play is commonly known as the Reverse X.

Description:
The area 2 spiker (No. 22 in Photos 6-14 a,b,c) runs to the setter and jumps as he is releasing the ball; meanwhile, the area 3 spiker is crossing behind the area 2 spiker for a backset. To begin the drill, the coach passes the ball to the setter from area 5 and the hitters run the Reverse X; the player who spikes shags the ball and returns it to the cart by the coach. The two blockers stay in from three to five minutes.

Coaching Tips:
The setter should call this play when the best quick hitter is in area 2. By concentrating two attackers in area 2 the area 4 spiker will usually be able to contend with only one blocker when the team is using the three-hitter attack.

Equipment and Personnel:
Six balls and a ballcart, a coach, and seven to twelve spikers.

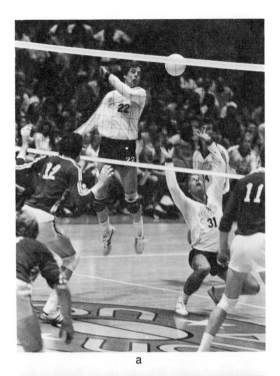

a

b

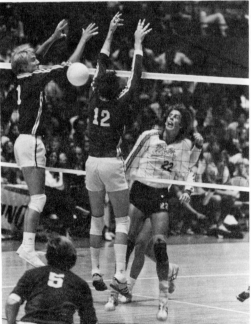

c

Photo 6-14   *The B Set. Karch (No. 31) squats to allow the ball to fall in a wavelike fashion to give the quick hitter (No. 22) time to jump in Photo 6-14a. The set is fast to prevent a tight block from forming and the hitter spikes through the seam in Photo 6-14c.* (Credit: George S. Yamashita)

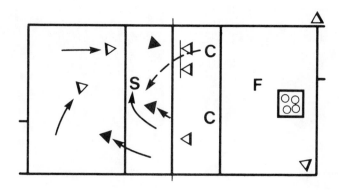

Figure 6-22   *Backing up the Spiker*

DRILL 6-22 BACKING UP THE SPIKER

Purpose:
To field balls that are blocked back into your court.

Description:
As the ball is set, the attacker's teammates back him up to prevent the blocked ball from hitting their court. If the spiker hits past the block, the coach in that area throws the ball into the attacker's court as if it were blocked. A feeder and a few shaggers keep the coaches supplied with balls.

Coaching Tip:
If the coaches are small, they can stand on tables and throw the balls down into the court to make it more realistic.

Equipment and Personnel:
Ten balls, one ballcart, two coaches, one or two feeders, two shaggers, and nine players.

Photo 6-15 *Backing up the Spiker. On a close set against a good block the players anticipate a stuff block and move close to the attacker.* Credit: (Dept. of Photography and Cinema The Ohio State University)

7

Scoring

**DRILL 7-1 QUICK TRANSITION
FROM AREA 2**

Purpose:
To score after blocking.

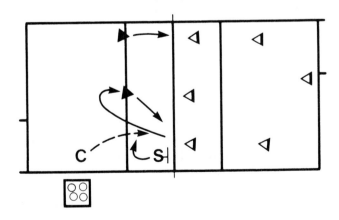

Figure 7-1 *Frontcourt Set to Area 4 or Quick Hitter*

Photo 7-1   *The High A. The fast high A set will defeat two blockers when they do not jump with the spiker.* (Credit: George S. Yamashita)

Description:

The setter and middle hitter block in area 2 and as they return to the floor, the coach lobs a ball to the setter who sets to the quick hitter (see Photo 7-1) or to the outside hitter. The six players on the other side defend and play it out until the ball hits the floor. Keep the players in the same position for three minutes and then rotate the line of three players.

Coaching Tip:

The coach should mix up the toss to the setter to simulate game conditions.

Equipment and Personnel:

Six balls, one ballcart, one coach, and nine players.

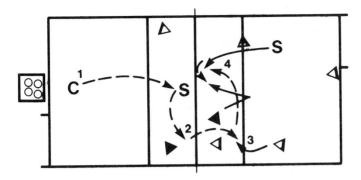

Figure 7-2   *Transition Set to Quick Hitter (Backcourt Setter)*

DRILL 7-2 QUICK TRANSITION FROM AREA 4

Purpose:
To beat the blockers with a quick set.

Description:
The coach throws the ball to the setter who sets to area 2 or 4. The spiker tries to side-out versus the defense who tries to score using a quick set to the middle attacker (see Photo 7-2). The rally is played out until the ball hits the floor.

Photo 7-2   *The Quick A. Singin Smith (No. 22) set to Steve Salmons before the blockers raised their hands in this 1979 photo of USC and UCLA. All six of the players shown have played with the USA team.* (Credit: Norm Schindler, ASUCLA)

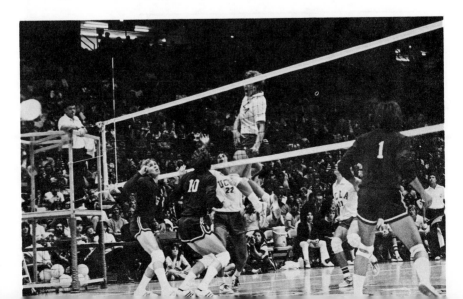

Coaching Tips:

If you have twelve players, keep your first team together as a unit. If there are fewer than twelve players, keep the setter and quick hitting combinations together.

Equipment and Personnel:

Eight balls, one ballcart, one coach, and nine to twelve players.

DRILL 7-3 QUICK HITTER
VERSUS TWO BLOCKERS

Purpose:

To teach the quick hitter to use a variety of shots when confronted with two blockers.

Description:

The setter and quick hitter jump in area 2 to simulate a block, and the coach throws the ball to the setter who delivers a one set to the quick hitter who is opposed by a two-man block. Three quick hitters can alternate spiking; each should shag the ball and return it to the cart after the spike. The blockers stay in for three to five minutes.

Coaching Tip:

A high flat spike to either corner is effective when confronted with two blockers on a quick set.

Equipment and Personnel:

Six balls, a cart, one coach, and six to nine players.

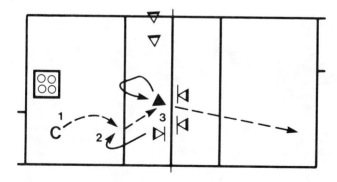

Figure 7-3 *Quick Hitter versus Two Blockers*

Photo 7-3 *The A versus Two Blockers. Good quick hitters command a lot of attention and occasionally draw two blockers when they have been scoring well. The best spike to use is the high flat shot in this situation.* (Credit: Norm Schindler, ASUCLA)

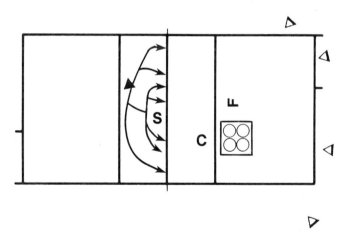

Figure 7-4 *Quick Transition Audibles*

DRILL 7-4 QUICK TRANSITION AUDIBLES

Purpose:
To give the quick hitter practice in calling for sets in transition.

Description:

The coach throws the ball to the hitter who passes to the setter and calls for a particular set, takes the proper route, and spikes the ball. The action is repeated for a specified number of sets or minutes depending on the maturity and condition of the hitter. Ten sets is a starting point and four minutes of rapid hitting should be the maximum for well-conditioned college players.

Coaching Tip:

The shaggers should yell encouragement.

Equipment and Personnel:

Four shaggers, a feeder, a coach, one hitter, and at least ten balls.

DRILL 7-5 AREA 6 TO AREA 4

Purpose:

To score on a high set from the backcourt by improving setting technique of players who defend area 6. At the same time the ability of spikers to stay behind the set in order to see the block will be emphasized.

Description:

The coach stands in area 1 and lobs a ball to the player in area 6 who either sets overhand or bump sets to the spiker in area 4. Two blockers oppose the spiker; these blockers work together for three to five minutes. After the spike, the hitter shags the ball and returns it to the cart. Then he goes to the spiking line. The setters alternate.

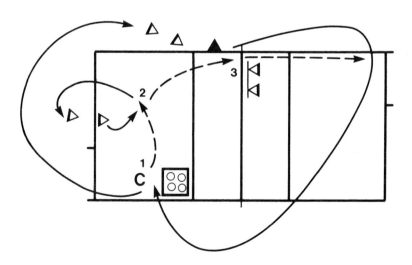

Figure 7-5 *Area 6 to Area 4*

Coaching Tips:
If all players play middle back and hit from the left, rotate from setter to spiker to shagger to setter. If players specialize in the middle back, then drill those players in area 6 exclusively.

Equipment and Personnel:
Six balls, one ballcart, one coach, and seven to twelve players.

DRILL 7-6 DIG AND SET TO AREA 4

Purpose:
To dig, set, and score after a deflected spike.

Description:
The coach stands on a table and spikes off the blockers to the backcourt. If the setter does not dig the ball, he sets the dig to area 4. The spiker tries to score and both teams play out the rally. If the setter digs, the closest players or the player with the best control sets.

Coaching Tip:
The better or closer to the net the dig is, the lower and faster the set. If the dig is deep, set high and give the spiker time to look over the defense.

Equipment and Personnel:
Eight balls, a table, ballcart, a coach, and twelve players.

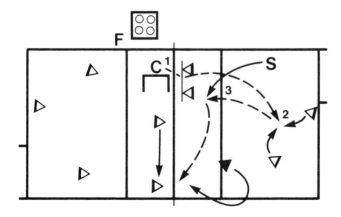

Figure 7-6   *Dig and Set to Area 4*

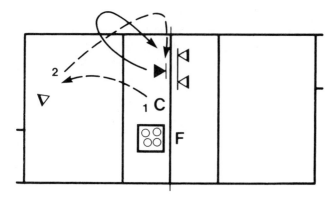

Figure 7-7 *Mock Block and Spike*

DRILL 7-7 MOCK, BLOCK AND SPIKE

Purpose:
To speed up the spikers' transition from blocking to spiking.

Description:
The coach calls "jump," and the spiker blocks as the coach throws the ball to the middle back player to set. After the spike, the hitter quickly assumes the blocking position and the drill is repeated.

Coaching Tip:
For endurance training use ten spikes apiece.

Equipment and Personnel:
Ten balls, a ballcart, one coach, and five to twelve players.

DRILL 7-8 BLOCK AND SET

Purpose:
To give the area 1 defender practice in passing the ball to the area 2 player who sets.

Description:
The coach stands on a table and spikes or dinks over the blocker to the area 1 defender (see Photo 7-4) who passes to area 2. The setter in area 2 sets to either spiker, and the team on the other side tries to prevent the score.

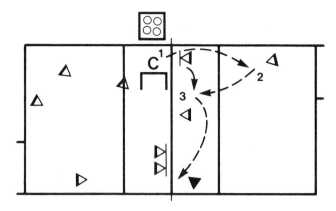

Figure 7-8   *Block and Set*

Photo 7-4   *Pass to Area 2. When the backcourt setter passes the ball, he should direct it to the area 2 blocker who will have two spikers to front set to.* (Credit: Norm Schindler, ASUCLA)

Coaching Tip:
The coach should alternate hard spikes and dinks to give the defenders a gamelike situation.

Equipment and Personnel:
Ten balls, a ballcart, one table, a coach, and ten to twelve players.

DRILL 7-9 AREA 5 TO AREA 2

Purpose:
To train the blocker in area 2 to make a quick transition from blocking to the attack.

Description:
The player in area 2 jumps on the coach's command and, as the blocker is returning to the floor, the coach throws the ball to the player in area 5 who sets to area 2. The spiker hits against two blockers who work together for three to five minutes. The spiker shags the ball and returns to the spiking line. The coach rotates the players groups from spiker to setter to blocker to spiker.

Coaching Tip:
If the player is setting on the run, he should attempt to set straight up and his forward momentum will carry the ball to area 2.

Equipment and Personnel:
Six balls, a cart, one coach, and eight to twelve players.

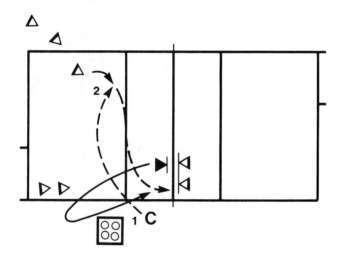

Figure 7-9   *Area 5 to Area 2*

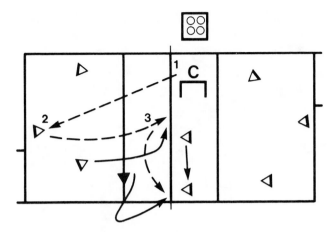

Figure 7-10   *Dig and Set to Area 2*

DRILL 7-10 DIG AND SET TO AREA 2

Purpose:
To combine digging and setting to score from area 2.

Description:
The coach stands on a table and spikes to any of the four defenders; the dig is set to the area 2 spiker who puts the ball away against five defenders. The right back player on the coach's side acts as the feeder to keep the coach supplied with balls. As usual, the drill continues until someone puts the ball away.

Coaching Tip:
The coach should spend equal time spiking from areas 2, 3, and 4 as this drill is used throughout the season.

Equipment and Personnel:
Eight balls, a cart, table, one coach, and nine to twelve players.

DRILL 7-11 BLOCK, DIG, AND SET TO AREA 2

Purpose:
To combine blocking, digging, and setting to score from area 2.

Description:
The coach stands on a table and spikes off the top of the block, and the defenders try to score from area 2 against a two-man block.

Photo 7-5   *Scoring from Area 2. Since our best spiker blocked in area 2, we spent many hours drilling the other setters and spikers to set in that area when the ball was dug.* (Credit: Norm Schindler, ASUCLA)

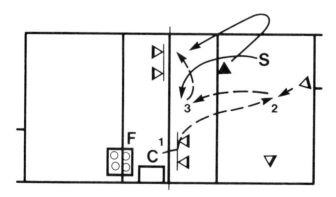

Figure 7-11   *Block, Dig, and Set to Area 2*

Coaching Tip:

Occasionally dink to the area 2 defender to make him dive to the center of the court so that he must quickly regain his feet and run outside to spike.

Equipment and Personnel:

Eight balls, a ballcart, table, one coach, and a minimum of nine players.

DRILL 7-12 SET EITHER WAY

Purpose:

To improve spiking sets from the backcourt.

Description:

The coach throws a ball to the player in area 6 who sets to either outside spiker who in turn attempts to score against a six-man defense. The defenders play it out and both teams try to put the ball away. Halfway through the drill flip-flop the front-row players with the back row on both sides of the court.

Coaching Tip:

Before playing league matches make sure that spikers know what the limits of their overhand setting abilities are. Some spikers with poor overhand setting capabilities should bump set all balls rather than use their hands.

Equipment and Personnel:

Six balls, one ballcart, one coach, and twelve players.

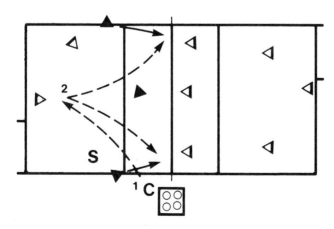

Figure 7-12   *Set Either Way*

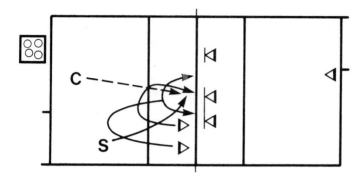

Figure 7-13   *Calling the Play in Transition (Area 2)*

DRILL 7-13 CALLING THE PLAY IN TRANSITION

Purpose:
To call an X or fake X when the ball is in the air.

Description:
The drill is run with two blockers in area 2 and a setter in area 1 facing three blockers and one, two, or three backcourt players. The coach yells "Jump" and the blockers go into the air; as they are returning to the floor, the coach throws the ball to area 2 or 3. The backcourt setter runs by the area 2 blocker and tells him "X" or "Fake" to determine his route. The middle blocker automatically comes for an A set.

Coaching Tip:
Specialize and only use two players to block in area 2. The spiker and setter will soon be able to coordinate the "call" if they practice continually with the same person.

DRILL 7-14 FREE BALL DRILL

Purpose:
To enable the team siding out to make a quick transition from the net to a new attack pattern when the defense returns their attack.

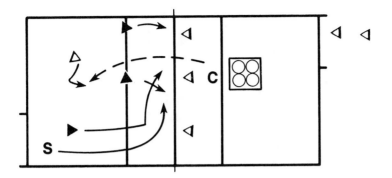

Figure 7-14   *Free Ball Drill*

Description:
The setter calls the play and the scoring team serves. If the three blockers do not block the ball back into the attacker's court, the coach throws the ball over the net and the side out team quickly runs another play. If the block puts the ball down in the opponent's court, the ball is dead and the side out team lines up for another serve and the action is repeated. If the spikers keep hitting by the block the coach throws balls over the net until the side out team is blocked.

Coaching Tip:
Have a prearranged free ball play that the hitters run when the setter calls ''Free''.

Equipment and Personnel:
Five or six players siding out; three blockers; two servers who double as shaggers, a coach, and a ballcart with ten balls.

DRILL 7-15 SCORING FROM THE BACKCOURT

Purpose:
To train the setters and spikers to score from the backcourt.

Description:
The coach starts the drill by tossing the ball to the frontcourt setter who sets at least half of the balls to the area 1 player. The area 1 player takes off behind the three meter line and contacts the set five to eight feet from the net. The setter attacks or sets the other two players about half the time. The six players on the other side attempt to dig the ball to their frontcourt setter and also attack

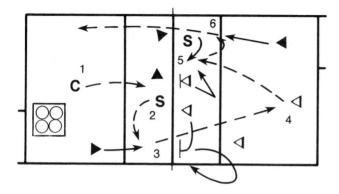

Figure 7-15 *Scoring from the Backcourt*

with their area 1 player half of the time. This keeps the blockers guessing and it is a game-like drill when the setter moves the ball to various attackers. The drill continues until the ball hits the floor and then the action is repeated.

Coaching Tips:

When the defenders dig the ball make sure the area 1 player calls a "D" to indicate he wants the set along the right sideline. If he wants the set in the middle of the court he should yell "Pipe".

Equipment and Personnel:

One cart, twelve balls, one coach, and ten or more players.

a

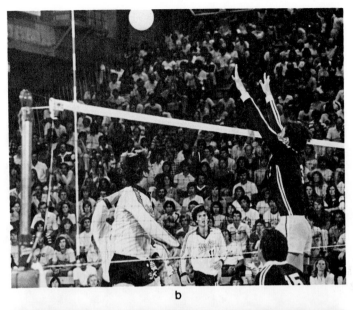

b

c

Photo 7-6   *Free Ball Play. When our opponents give us an easy or "free ball" to play at UCLA, we usually use the Right X play shown above. In Photo 7-6a Steve Gulnac (No. 30) has the opposing middle blocker jumping with him as No. 15 waits for the area 2 hitter who has not yet committed to the X pattern. In Photo 7-6b the middle blocker is still in the air and screens his teammate (No. 15) out of the play as the blockers watch the X set loop over the quick hitter. In Photo 7-6c the right-side blocker makes a valiant but unsuccessful effort to block the crossing attacker.* (Credit: Norm Schindler, ASUCLA)

8

Team Defense

DRILL 8-1 ROTATION DEFENSE

Purpose:
To defend against an opponent who can hit a strong line shot.

Description:
The coach tosses the ball to the setter who delivers the ball on top of the net to the area 4 attacker. The end blocker (see Photo 8-1) keeps his hand between the ball and the sideline; the area 1 and 4 defenders move in for a dink

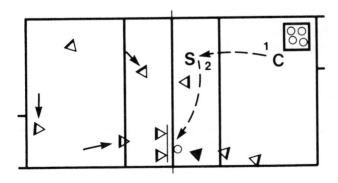

Figure 8-1 *Rotation Defense*

Photo 8-1 *Turning the Ball In. On a close set the outside blocker must keep his hand between the ball and the antenna; this is commonly known as "turning it in."* (Credit: Norm Schindler, ASUCLA)

shot; the area 6 defender moves behind the seam of the block on the endline; and the area 5 defender plays for a crosscourt deflection. The defenders try to score against the three blockers on the coach's side of the net. The spiker on the coach's side shags the ball and goes to the end of the spiking line.

Coaching Tip:
The area 1 defender has to be ready to move to his right to field balls wiped off the blockers.

Equipment and Personnel:
Six balls, a cart, one coach, and nine to twelve players.

DRILL 8-2 DINK ROTATION

Purpose:
To teach the backcourt players defensive positions in a rotating defense.

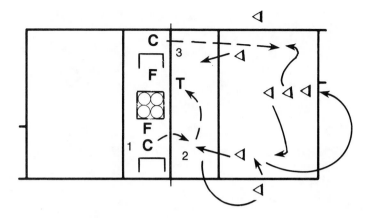

Figure 8-2 *Dink Rotation Drill*

Description:

The three backcourt players stand in their starting defensive positions. At UCLA the area 6 digger is ten feet from the endline in the center of the court and wing diggers are twelve feet from the net a few feet from the sideline. The coach stands on a table and slaps the ball to simulate a set coming to him; at this signal the digger in front of him moves towards the net to get the dink shot and the middle back player rotates to the corner to defend the unprotected area of the court. (Please note that rotational defenses expect the middle blocker to stop or deflect spikes to area 6. If this is not the case with your team do not use this drill.) The coach dinks or spikes the ball down the line. At this point the coach on the other sideline slaps the ball and the drill is repeated on the other side. The players rotate after every movement but only practice in the defensive area or areas the coach has assigned to them.

Coaching Tips:

The player taking the dink shot must stay in a low position with the feet spread wide ready to react in any direction for the dink shot; this player has no responsibility for a spike and must be ready to sprawl forward as shown in photo 8-2.

Equipment and Personnel:

Two tables, one ballcart with twelve to twenty balls, two coaches, two feeders, one target player, six to nine diggers, and a few sluggers.

Photo 8-2   *Dink Recovery. Using the back of the hand is called the "pancake dig"; it has become a popular technique in recent years.* (Credit: Norm Schindler, ASUCLA)

DRILL 8-3 THE J MOVE

Purpose:
To defend the corners of the court against a crosscourt hit in the rotation defense.

Description:
The coach stands on a table and slaps the ball to start the defender quickly side stepping to the corner using a route that resembles the shape of the letter J. This drill is designed for the middle back defense where the area 1 and 5 defenders usually start about twelve feet from the net to protect against dink shots and retrieve block rebounds. Normally these defenders do not get deep enough to defend the corner unless specifically drilled to do so. The coach on the stand quickly spikes to the crosscourt corner after slapping the ball and the digger directs the spike to the target player. The digger then returns to the original starting position as the other coach slaps the ball and hits to the other digger. Two players

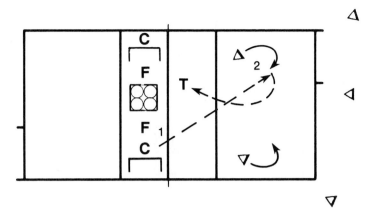

Figure 8-3   *The J Move*

stay on the court for a specified number of digs or minutes. We run four groups of two through this drill in under twenty minutes giving each group at least four minutes on the court. While waiting the other players shag, feed, and act as the target.

Coaching Tips:

The diggers should stay low so that they do not react to balls that would fly out of bounds. We prefer that our players dig with one knee touching the floor because this technique seems to improve their ball control.

Equipment and Personnel:

Two tables, one ballcart with twelve to twenty balls, two coaches, and six to eight players.

DRILL 8-4 MIDDLE BACK ROTATION

Description:

Three players line up in single file in area 6 with the first player ten feet from the endline. The coach or designate is on a table and spikes the ball down the sideline. In the rotation defense the wing diggers are responsible for the dink shot so the middle back must rotate quickly to the sideline and stop before the ball is spiked. As the first digger moves to the left the next digger moves to the middle back starting position (at UCLA we start ten feet from the endline) and then rapidly moves to the right to dig a spike from the other coach. The third player moves to the starting position and then moves to his left. With an odd number of players the diggers will alternate left and right every time they go through the line. Usually every player on the team plays middle back except the setter. At

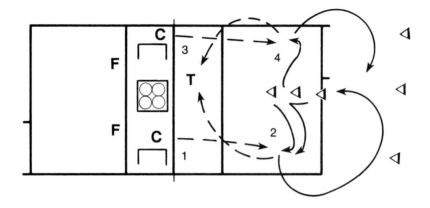

Figure 8-4 Middle Back Rotation

UCLA we make every spiker go through this drill. Three groups of three work best with three shaggers rotating to diggers and then to the target player and two feeders.

Coaching Tip:

Have the person spiking slap the ball to signal that the set is on the way; at that signal the digger begins the rotation to the sideline. The digger should use a slide step to move so he will not be caught in a stride position when the ball is spiked.

Equipment and Personnel:

One ballcart, twelve balls, two tables or stands, two spikers, two feeders and a target player, three diggers, and three shaggers.

DRILL 8-5 VERSUS A FOUR SET

Purpose:

To defense the spike of a low fast set (four) to the area 4 spiker when one or two blockers are defending.

Description:

Two spiking lines are formed in areas 2 and 4, and the setter sets forward approximately two out of three times. The ball is passed by the coach from area 1. After the spiker hits the ball, she shags it and returns the ball to the cart and goes to the end of the spiking line. When the middle blocker is late, she should defend against the dink shot and *never* come off the net to dig a hard-spiked ball. The area 6, 5, and 4 diggers play for a crosscourt shot and the area 1 digger for a line shot or dink.

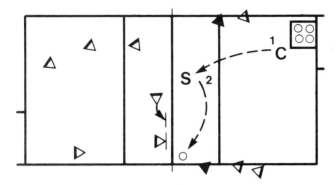

Figure 8-5   *Versus a Four Set*

Photo 8-3   *The Four Set. The middle blocker is often late on a quick four set so the end blocker must move toward the center of the court and slide her arms toward the middle blocker.* (Credit: Norm Schindler, ASUCLA)

Coaching Tips:

The lower and faster the set, the farther inside the area 2 blocker should move. The lower the level of play, the more the ball is spiked crosscourt and the more the block should move inside. Inexperienced spikers make more mistakes when they try to spike line.

Equipment and Personnel:

Six balls, a cart, twelve players, and a coach.

DRILL 8-6 VERSUS A FIVE SET

Purpose:

To defense the spike of a low fast set (five) to the area 2 spiker when one or two blockers are defending.

Description:

Always work on defending against five and four sets during the same drill so the middle blocker can work on reading the setter and the diggers can adjust to a late middle blocker; a two-man block; or a one-man block. Simply tell the setter where to deliver the most balls if you wish to put emphasis on defending the five or four set. This drill is run the same way as 8-5.

Coaching Tip:

When the area 2 spiker approaches the net at an angle, expect a crosscourt spike.

Equipment and Personnel:

Six balls, a cart, twelve players, and a coach.

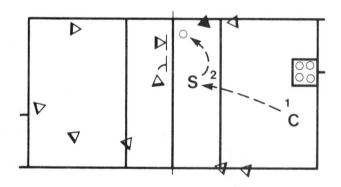

Figure 8-6 *Versus a Five Set*

Photo 8-4 *The Five Set. Since the spiker (No. 29) took a straight approach, the defense expected a spike down the line and the end blocker lined up slightly outside the spiker in good position.* (Credit: Norm Schindler, ASUCLA)

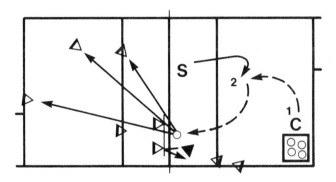

Figure 8-7 *Versus a High Set*

DRILL 8-7 VERSUS A HIGH SET

Purpose:
To defense the spike of a high set to an outside spiker.

Description:
The coach throws the ball to the setter somewhere in the backcourt so that he will have to deliver a high set to the outside attacker. Since there will always be at least a two-man block on a high set, only one spiking line may be used. Since most high sets go to area 4, this side should be emphasized most in defensive drills.

Photo 8-5   *The High Set. Three blockers are often effective against a predictable high set.* (Credit: Ohio State University)

Coaching Tip:
When the blockers get used to blocking fast sets, they will have to tell each other to "Wait" on a high set and then say "Now" to coordinate their jump.

Equipment and Personnel:
Six balls, a cart, nine to twelve players, and a coach.

DRILL 8-8 VERSUS A QUICK SET

Purpose:
To introduce the defense for the quick set.

Description:
One spiking line hits quick sets versus a full defense who attempts to score. Only one blocker will block the quick hitter during this drill. The area 1 and 5 diggers start on the attack line versus élite players as diagrammed and start progressively toward the back line as the potential ability of the quick hitter diminishes. In other words, if the quick hitter cannot spike inside the attack line, move deeper into the court. The coach varies the passes along the net.

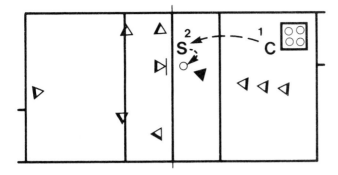

Figure 8-8   *Versus a Quick Set*

Photo 8-6   *Versus the Quick Hitter. On a good pass the entire defense prepares for a quick set to the middle attacker. Notice that the area one and five defenders are close to the attack line.* (Credit: Ohio State University)

Coaching Tip:

The blocker must have his arms extended before he leaves the floor, or the quick hitter will beat him.

Equipment and Personnel:

Six balls, a cart, nine to twelve players, and a coach.

DRILL 8-9 VERSUS THE RIGHT X

Purpose:

To defend against the A and the X set.

Description:

The coach throws the ball to the setter who sets the A or the X set shown in Photo 8-7b. The blockers try to read the setter and all three get up with the X set if possible. The area 5 player covers the dink when the area 2 blocker is up on the X set.

Coaching Tip:

The area 4 blocker can jump with the quick hitter (No. 11 in Photo 8-7b) and still jump again with the X man if he does not drop his arms.

Equipment and Personnel:

Six balls, a cart, eleven to twelve players, and a coach.

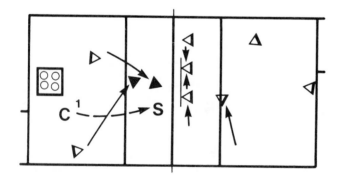

Figure 8-9   *Versus the Right X*

a

b

Photo 8-7 *The X Set. No. 1 is shown in Photo 8-7a on the first step of his approach as the setter contacts the ball. In Photo 8-7b the ball is reaching the apex of its flight as the spiker prepares to take off. The set should be higher for slower players.* (Credit: Norm Schindler, ASUCLA)

DRILL 8-10 VERSUS THE FAKE X

Purpose:
To defend against the quick set and back two set.

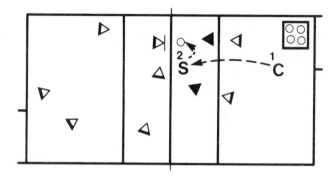

Figure 8-10   *Versus a Back Two Set (Fake X)*

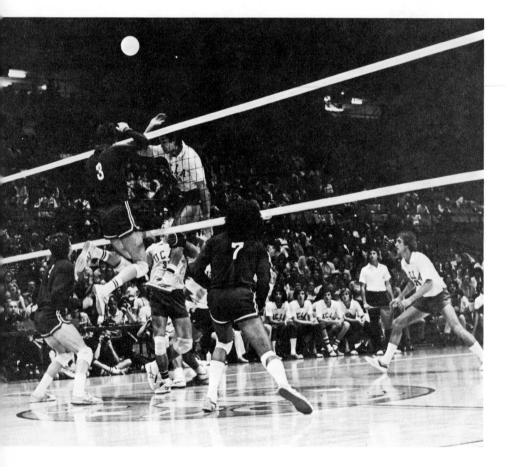

Photo 8-8   *The Fake X Set. The middle blocker has responsibility for the quick hitter on the fake X pattern because the area 4 blocker must wait for the spiker running the fake X route. Players must become proficient at one-on-one blocking to stop this play.* (Credit: Norm Schindler, ASUCLA)

Description:

The middle blocker (No. 3) often jumps with the quick hitter as shown in Photo 8-8. When he is fooled, the area 4 blocker must block the fake X set by himself. When the middle blocker is not fooled, the area 5 digger moves behind the end blocker for a dink shot; when there is one blocker, the area 5 digger should stay back as shown in the diagram.

Coaching Tip:

The area 4 blocker must constantly talk to the middle blocker to let him know which route the right-side spiker is taking. When he sees him running the X pattern, he shouts "Cross"; when he cuts back to the sideline, he shouts "Fake." This drill can be run with blockers only, or a full defense.

Equipment and Personnel:

Eight balls, a cart, one coach, and nine to twelve players.

DRILL 8-11 VERSUS A C SET

Purpose:

To defeat the fast set delivered five to eight feet from the setter.

Description:

The key defender is the area 2 blocker who must align himself directly in front of the middle hitter who will usually cut this set back to area 1. This is a tough assignment for the area 2 blocker because his primary responsibility is still the outside hitter. The setter should set fours to the outside attacker during this drill so that the area 2 blocker can experience moving to cover the middle attacker, then recovering to move outside.

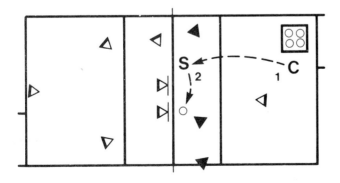

Figure 8-11 *Versus a C Set*

Photo 8-9   *The C Set. The middle player has to watch the quick hitter's route and the setter to see if he drops his hands when delivering this set. If he waits until the ball is delivered without observing the above cues, he will be late on the block.* (Credit: Jorgen A. Sabarz)

Coaching Tip:
The area 2 blocker should start ten feet from the right sideline when a team likes to run three sets.

Equipment and Personnel:
Six balls, a cart, one coach, and nine to twelve players.

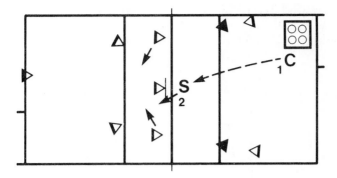

Figure 8-12 *Versus the Dump*

DRILL 8-12 VERSUS THE DUMP

Purpose:
To defense the setter attacking the second ball.

Description:
The coach throws balls to the setter that she can set or dump (see Photos 8-10, a,b). She sets to either of the spikers or attacks the ball herself. The middle blocker is primarily responsible for the setter attacking unless the ball is passed close to a sideline. The end blockers are responsible for any block deflections and dumps and step away from the net as shown in Photo 8-10b. The defense attempts to score and the setter and two spikers block the scoring attempt and play it out until the rally is concluded.

Coaching Tip:
The middle blocker should keep her hands above her shoulder so that she can quickly extend them when the setter attacks.

Equipment and Personnel:
Six balls, a cart, one coach, and nine to twelve players.

DRILL 8-13 VERSUS A HIGH MIDDLE SET

Purpose:
To defend against the high set in the middle.

Photo 8-10a and b *Setter Dump. Good setters learn to dump with their left hand while facing area 4 as shown above. This tactic holds the middle blocker and gives the two attackers a one-on-one situation.* (Credit: Norm Schindler, ASUCLA)

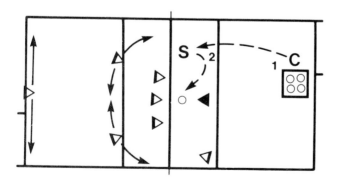

Figure 8-13 *Versus a High Middle Set*

Description:

The coach tosses balls to the setter who has the option of dumping, setting outside, or setting a high ball to the middle attacker. This keeps the blockers "honest" and is a gamelike situation. When the set is to the middle, all three blockers defend. The area 1 and 5 defenders cover the dink shot and the area 6 defender is responsible for block deflections. The defense plays it out and tries to score while the setter and two attackers transition to blocking.

Coaching Tip:

The middle back defender must "read" the spiker and move in the direction of his armswing. Most good spikers try to hit off the end blocker toward the area 5 corner when confronted with a three-person block.

Equipment and Personnel:

Six balls, a cart, one coach, and nine to twelve players.

DRILL 8-14 VERSUS AN INSIDE SET

Purpose:

To teach the middle blocker to position the block while the end blocker moves to him.

Description:

The coach passes to the setter who delivers a back two set to the spikers in the attacking line. The end blocker moves to the middle blocker and the area 5 digger moves behind the blockers (No. 1 in Photo 8-11) for the dink shot. The defense tries to score while the attackers transition to blockers. The player who spiked the first ball shags and returns to the end of the spiking line.

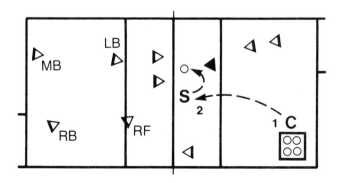

Figure 8-14 *Versus an Inside Set*

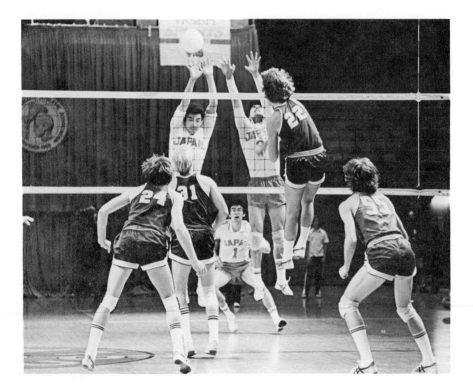

Photo 8-11 *Two-Man Block. On an inside set the end blocker must move in and close the seam between the blockers as the Japanese All Stars demonstrate here.* (Credit: Norm Schindler, ASUCLA)

Coaching Tip:
Occasionally have the setter deliver to the area 4 spiker so the middle blocker will react in a gamelike situation.

Equipment and Personnel:
Six balls, a cart, one coach, and nine to twelve players.

DRILL 8-15 VERSUS WIDE SETS

Purpose:
To teach the defense to rotate into the pending area of attack.

Description:
The coach stands behind the middle blocker and tosses the ball outside the antenna, forcing the spiker to hit crosscourt. The blockers move in and everyone rotates into the possible area of attack. The players in areas 2 and 3 and the spiker transition to blocking if the defense digs the spike.

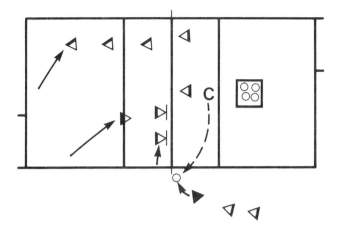

Figure 8-15   *Versus Wide Sets*

Photo 8-12   *Blocking a Wide Set. When the ball is set outside the antenna, blockers have a tendency to position their hands toward the hitter and block the ball out of bounds instead of positioning the hands toward the middle back of the court as the blockers in the photograph have done.* (Credit: Stan Troutman)

Coaching Tip:

The blockers must have their hands facing the middle back of the opponents' court to keep the blocked spike inbounds.

Equipment and Personnel:

Six balls, one cart, one coach, and nine to twelve players.

9

Conditioning

DRILL 9-1 SPIKE, RECOVER, SPIKE

Purpose:
To increase endurance while improving spiking skills.

Description:
The coach throws the ball to the setter and the spiker tries to put the ball away against a two-person block. The extra players shag balls and return them to the feeder. After ten spikes the player rests while another player spikes ten balls. The resting spiker makes sure that the blocked balls are cleared from under the active spiker's feet. The drill is repeated two to three times depending on the condition of the spikers.

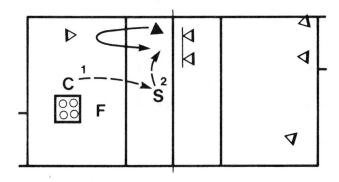

Figure 9-1 *Spike, Recover, Spike*

Coaching Tip:
This type of interval training is time-consuming, particularly with large groups. If a team does not have adequate gym time, interval training can be done off the court using a series of 70-yard sprints from a jogging start.

Equipment and Personnel:
Ten balls, a cart, one coach, and eight to twelve players.

DRILL 9-2 SPIKE AND DIVE

Purpose:
To increase endurance while working on the quick hit and dive.

Description:
The coach at the net tosses a quick set for the spiker and as he returns to the floor, the coach behind him tosses him a ball to dive for. The player then regains his feet and goes to the end of the line; meanwhile the player acting as the target (T) returns the ball to the feeder in the backcourt. The shaggers on the other side of the net return the ball to the spiking line feeder. Ten spikes and ten dives with five to six players moving through the drill in a rapid manner consist of one set. Each player can go through the drill one, two, or three times depending on the intensity of the training session and technical and physical ability.

Coaching Tip:
The spiker should keep his eye on the ball as shown in Photo 9-1 and dig it high in the air.

Equipment and Personnel:
Ten balls, two coaches, and ten to twelve players.

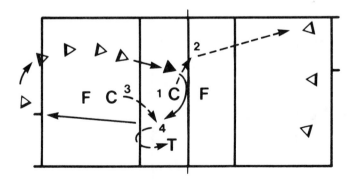

Figure 9-2   *Spike and Dive*

Photo 9-1 *Diving Save. Anyone who is close to the ball should try to recover it. In this photo two players are diving for the same ball, and one of them is already attempting to hit it back to the setter (No. 22) who has his hand raised and is calling for the ball.* (Credit: Norm Schindler, ASUCLA)

DRILL 9-3 REPETITIVE SPIKES AND BLOCKS WITH A PASS

Purpose:
To increase two players' endurance while working on another player's passing technique.

Description:
The coach serves to the player in area 5, and the setter backsets his pass to the area 2 spiker while the area 4 player on the coach's side blocks. After blocking, the area 4 player receives a set from the coach and the area 2 player blocks. If the ball is not dug by the area 5 player, the coach serves another ball to area 5 and the drill is repeated; if the area 5 player does dig the ball, the setter delivers a backset and the drill is repeated. After ten spikes and blocks the area 4 spiker should be replaced; he can come back in after the next player is done.

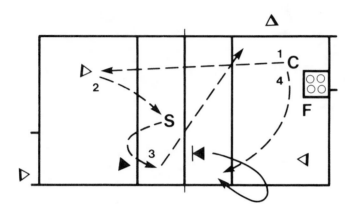

Figure 9-3   *Repetitive Spikes and Blocks with a Pass*

Coaching Tip:
The starting player who is the poorest passer should pass during the entire drill from his weakest passing position.

Equipment and Personnel:
Ten balls, a cart, one coach, and eight to twelve players.

DRILL 9-4 REPETITIVE DEEP SPIKES

Purpose:
To increase endurance and improve the ability to spike deep sets.

Description:
The coach stands in area 3 and alternately lobs sets to areas 4 and 2 about ten feet from the net. The spikers try to put the ball away against the diggers in areas 5, 6, and 1. A player (T) stands in front of the net to serve as a target for the diggers and to prevent a ball from going under the spikers' feet. The target player puts balls in the cart for the coach; all other players not involved in the drill serve as shaggers.

Coaching Tip:
The coach should lob the sets far enough from the net so that the back-court players have a chance to dig the ball. This distance will vary according to the ability of the spikers.

Equipment and Personnel:
Ten balls, one cart, a coach, and eight to twelve players.

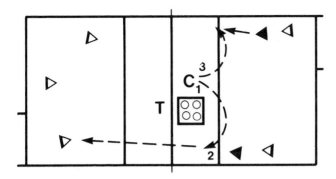

Figure 9-4 *Repetitive Deep Spikes*

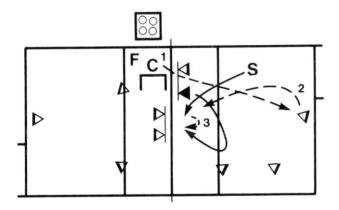

Figure 9-5 *Quick Hitter Block and Spike Repetitively*

DRILL 9-5 QUICK HITTER BLOCK AND SPIKE REPETITIVELY

Purpose:
To increase endurance and to transition quickly from blocking to attacking.

Description:
The coach stands on a table and spikes balls off the blockers' hands to the backcourt. The middle blocker drops off the net as the ball is dug to the setter and approaches and spikes a quick set. Two blockers oppose the quick hitter and if they block the ball back into the spiker's court, his teammates pass the block rebound to the setter and the quick hitter spikes again. If the defense digs the ball, they try to score using their quick hitter. When the ball is dead, the coach hits another ball at the blockers.

Coaching Tips:

Quick hitters use a one-, two-, three-, or four-step approach on the transition from blocking to spiking, depending on the amount of time they have. The important point is that they jump as the setter is contacting the ball.

Equipment and Personnel:

Ten balls, a cart, a table, a coach, and twelve players.

DRILL 9-6 AREA 2 VERSUS AREA 4 SPIKER

Purpose:

To increase players' endurance while working on spiking and blocking skills in a highly competitive drill.

Description:

The coach throws the ball to the setter and the spiker in area 4 tries to put the ball away against a full defense. If the defense digs the ball, they set it to their area 2 spiker and the player in area 4 blocks. The play continues until the ball hits the floor. The coach on the side of the net that lost the rally tosses the ball into play to initiate the next rally. A point is scored on each rally and the team that gets to ten points first wins. The players rotate until everyone who spikes and blocks in area 2 and 4 participates in those positions.

Coaching Tips:

Because this is an endurance drill, the coach must put the ball into play as soon as the ball is dead so there is no time to rest. To insure intense competition, match up first team players opposite each other in area 2 and 4.

Equipment and Personnel:

As many balls as the team possesses divided into two ballcarts, two coaches, and twelve players.

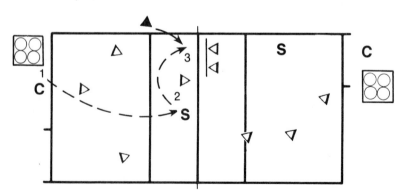

Figure 9-6 *Area 2 Versus Area 4 Spiker*